Selecting a Thinking Skills Program

HOW TO ORDER THIS BOOK

BY PHONE: 800-233-9936 or 717-291-5609, 8AM–5PM Eastern Time

BY FAX: 717-295-4538

BY MAIL: Order Department
Technomic Publishing Company, Inc.
851 New Holland Avenue, Box 3535
Lancaster, PA 17604, U.S.A.

BY CREDIT CARD: American Express, VISA, MasterCard

Selecting a Thinking Skills Program

Joyce Ragland Banks, Ed.D.

TECHNOMIC
PUBLISHING CO., INC.
LANCASTER · BASEL

Selecting a Thinking Skills Program

a TECHNOMIC® publication

Published in the Western Hemisphere by
Technomic Publishing Company, Inc.
851 New Holland Avenue
Box 3535
Lancaster, Pennsylvania 17604 U.S.A.

Distributed in the Rest of the World by
Technomic Publishing AG

Printed in the United States of America
10 9 8 7 6 5 4 3 2 1

Main entry under title:
Selecting a Thinking Skills Program

A Technomic Publishing Company book
Bibliography: p.
Index: p. 109

Library of Congress Card No. 90-72123
ISBN No. 87762-788-6

To Dale and Alana Banks
thanks is such a small word for
extensive encouragement and patience.

and

To Ella Ragland, my mother, whose advice
"Get out and make something of yourself"
still echoes in my ears.

TABLE OF CONTENTS

FOREWORD

Joyce Banks has written a book busy school practitioners will relish. It is a book about thinking skills. More importantly, it is about how to select among the half dozen or more that can be implemented "off the shelf." She patiently differentiates among the competing claims, traces the histories and concepts, and presents them in a refreshing and understandable way, remarkably free from the heavy doses of theory and "researchese" that permeate this field.

There are few teachers, principals, superintendents, or board members who have not been dismayed by the slavish emphasis on rote work and memorization brought on by statewide competency assessment and the continued use of standardized achievement tests as the "only way" to measure learning in the schools. "Thinking skills" offers a way to improve achievement but more than that, an alternative. The use of a "thinking skills" program goes beyond memorization and touches the heart of learning where it is simply important to know something for the joy of discovery.

Yet not all "thinking skills" programs are alike, as Banks clearly shows. Some will attain different ends and some work better in some situations than others. Knowing which program(s) to select for your school is what this book is about.

I believe the practitioners who take the time to get into Banks' book will find it extremely useful as a practical guide to the appropriate selection of a thinking skills program. It may well be the single most important decision ever made at your school.

Professor and Head　　　　　　　　　　　　　　FENWICK W. ENGLISH
Educational Administration
University of Cincinnati, Ohio

PREFACE

The purpose of this book is to present information regarding thinking skills programs in such a way as to be easily readable for both the practitioner and the layman.

School executives (identified variously in the U.S. and Canada as superintendents, directors, heads, principals) are in the unique position of needing to read and interpret educational research and then translate, i.e., explain the implications of such research to school boards, parent groups, and, on occasion perhaps, to students. School executives are extremely busy individuals. A high school principal once described his role as analogous to a fireman who has to put out a number of small fires daily, with occasional major fires springing up when least expected. This principal has little time for reading and translating the vast amounts of research available regarding the large number of issues in education today. This book is intended as a practical resource tool for the busy school executive.

Teachers are frequently initiators of new curricula. This is particularly true with regard to thinking skills programs. Many schools have adopted thinking skills programs as a result of positive experiences related by individual teachers trying out a program that they had heard about from colleagues at other schools.

At the present time, the ordinary "person on the street" has likely heard of the "Nation at Risk" report (and perhaps others) linked with the phrase "critical thinking skills." Various news reports have followed on television, radio, newspapers, and even in household magazines, decrying the lack of teaching for thinking in schools. Parent groups, including school boards, are thus somewhat familiar with the need to teach thinking skills as part of the educational program. They are less likely to know what various programs are available, how and what each program purports to teach, how to calculate long-term costs in balance to the benefits of various programs, or whether to initiate their own district-wide "generic" approaches to the teaching of thinking skills. If laypersons were asked to define generic thinking skills, creative thinking skills, or critical thinking skills, most would not be able readily to do so. A few would perhaps say something about involving problem solving, but even this response would probably be only vaguely conceptualized.

This book examines some of the most widely used thinking skills programs in terms of (a) research summaries, (b) the types of schools and classrooms using these programs, (c) implementation costs and procedures, and (d) the "generic" thinking skills approach.

Chapter 2 includes a sample proposal which could be used as a guide for a presentation to a school board or parent–teacher group by a school teacher or executive desiring to initiate a thinking skills program in his/her school.

Chapters 3 through 7 provide extensive information regarding the four most rigorous of thinking skills programs, Philosophy for Children, Instrumental Enrichment, CoRT, and Structure of the Intellect.

Chapter 7 includes information regarding some of the newer programs that have less research to date regarding their effectiveness than do the programs in the preceding chapters.

Chapter 8 contains five editorials regarding different approaches to teaching thinking skills, including viewpoints from an elementary principal, a high school mathematics teacher, a college English teacher and a resource (special education) teacher.

ACKNOWLEDGEMENTS

James Beamer, Associate Professor, Department of Curriculum Studies, College of Education, University of Saskatchewan.

Lattie Collins, III, East Tennessee State University, Johnson City, Tennessee.

Patricia Cunningham, Teachers Assistant, Special Education, Laclede County R-1 Schools, Conway, Missouri.

Allan Guy, Associate Professor, Educational Leadership, College of Education, University of Saskatchewan.

Rita Hlady, Catalyst Teacher for Gifted Education, Saskatoon, Saskatchewan Public Schools.

William Pafford, Chair, Curriculum and Instruction, East Tennessee State University, Johnson City, Tennessee.

Michael Roberts, former Curriculum Director, University City Public Schools, St. Louis, Missouri.

University City Public School Teachers: Mary Batiste, Sylvia Bonner, Becky Brooks, Pat Dugan, Marilyn Levinson, Mary Long, Nancy Maebed, Nancy Mueller, Stephanie Ross, Jean Ann Staley, Eleanor Thomas.

Why Thinking Skills in the Curriculum?

1983: The timing of the news release surrounding the "A Nation at Risk" document was masterful! Those in the media business describe those days when there are no major worldwide conflicts, no new episodes in current wars, no man-made or natural disasters, etc. as "slow" news days. Slow news days are when documents such as "A Nation at Risk" are given the attention they deserve by national and international news organizations. If, for example, the "A Nation at Risk" report had been released close to an event such as the Challenger disaster or the shooting of President Reagan, the report would have gone largely unnoticed. But the timing was, by all indications, carefully planned, and the press coverage was all that a Secretary of Education could anticipate in his wildest dreams. Even the title was masterfully planned for modern media coverage. A title such as "Implications of Modern Societal Needs and the School" would have said the same thing without the emotional aspect of a term like "Risk." The point is, the report made news and has had an impact throughout North American educational institutions.

On the matter of teaching thinking skills the report indicates:

> . . . a problem, if schools emphasize such rudiments as reading and computation at the expense of other essential skills such as comprehension, analysis, solving problems, and drawing conclusions . . . many seventeen-year-olds do not possess the "higher" order intellectual skills we should expect of them . . . nearly forty percent cannot draw inferences from written material; only twenty percent can write a persuasive essay, and only one-third can solve a mathematics problem requiring several steps.

In reference to the goal of teaching thinking skills:

> . . . all children by virtue of their own efforts, competently guided, can hope to attain the mature and informed judgment needed to secure gain-

ful employment and to manage their own lives, thereby serving not only their own interests but also the progress of society itself.

The irony of the situation is that when the document is examined in comparison to many previous reports and research, it is easy to conclude that "A Nation at Risk" contained very little new information. For example, Horace Mann (1838), in a report to the Massachusetts State Board of Education, decried the lack of students' abilities to solve problems. John Dewey (1909) said, "The very importance of thought for life makes necessary its control by education because of its natural tendency to go astray, and because social influences exist that tend to form habits of thought leading to inadequate and erroneous beliefs." The National Education Association's (1987) Educational Policies Commission Report included as an "imperative . . . all youth need to grow in their ability to think rationally, to express their thoughts clearly, and to read and listen with understanding."

Henchy and Burgess (1987, p. 199) have identified similar reports in the United Kingdom and Canada: 1983 in Great Britain, a governmental report entitled "Teaching Quality"; 1985, Great Britain, "White Paper on Better Schools"; British Columbia, "Let's Talk about Schools"; Saskatchewan, "New Directions"; Manitoba, "Pour une education de qualité"; Alberta, "Secondary Education"; Quebec, "The Estates General on the Quality of Education."

The list goes on. Some of the more prominent reports are summarized below.

1980s U.S. REPORTS SUPPORTING TEACHING THINKING SKILLS

1983: Academic Preparation for College

New York: The College Board, a non-profit organization consisting of 2,500 colleges, schools, school systems, and educational associations.

Reasoning Skills Needed:

- the ability to identify and formulate problems, as well as the ability to propose and evaluate ways to solve them
- the ability to recognize and use inductive and deductive reasoning and to recognize fallacies in reasoning
- the ability to draw reasonable conclusions from information

found in various sources, whether written, spoken, or displayed in tables and graphs, and to defend one's conclusions rationally
- the ability to comprehend, develop, and use concepts and generalizations
- the ability to distinguish between fact and opinion

1985: Critical Thinking: Its Nature, Measurement, and Improvement

Robert Sternberg. There is an ususual amount of consensus among eductors regarding the importance of including critical thinking skills in all aspects of curriculum.

1986: First Lessons

William Bennett, in the role of U.S. Secretary of Education, reporting to Congress:

- Children can learn amazing things if presented in language they fathom and in ways that engage their lively minds and imagination . . . the principle goals of education are to build for every child a strong foundation for further education, for democratic citizenship, and for eventual entry into responsible adulthood.

1987: Learning to Be Literate in America: Reading, Writing, and Reasoning

A. Applebee, J. Langer, and I. Mullis: . . . literacy is the ability to read and write, and to reason about what one reads or writes.

SELECTED CANADIAN REPORTS

1987: Between Past and Future

N. Henchey and D. Burgess, (p. 85) regarding Quebec elementary and secondary education in transition: there are few ideas in the curriculum about how to teach creative and logical thinking, new skills for using modern information technologies to find and reduce the quantity of information now increasingly available to all . . . that may be required for survival in decades to come.

1988: Common Essential Learnings

Saskatchewan Education (the provincial department of education) calls for the teaching of both critical and creative thinking skills across the curriculum in all schools in the province of Saskatchewan, including Adult Education programs: . . . must develop analytical skills, teaching students not just what to remember but also how to think critically and independently.

THE UNITED KINGDOM

1983: Education 2000

B. Thwaites and C. Wysock-Wright, editors (pp. 36, 41) include reasoning as: a necessary survival skill and that further education in technology . . . will involve intellectually demanding skills: the ability to identify, examine and solve problems, use a variety of materials, and in so doing stretch to the full the pupil's inventive and innovatory powers. The pupil thereby acquires the capability to synthesize these skills.

In regard to a core curriculum for 14–18-year-olds, include skills and concepts associated with investigation, inquiry, and judgment.

A PARTIAL LISTING OF EDUCATORS SUPPORTING THE TEACHING OF THINKING SKILLS

Carl Beretier (1985), professor in the Centre for Applied Cognitive Science, Ontario Institute for Studies in Education, Toronto, Ontario.

Ernest Boyer (1985), president of The Carnegie Foundation for the Advancement of Teaching and former U.S. Commissioner of Education.

Robert H. Ennis (1985), professor of Philosophy of Education at the University of Illinois, director of the Illinois Critical Thinking Project, and coauthor of the "Cornell Critical Thinking Test" levels X and 2.

Edward M. Glaser (1985), president of the Human Interaction Research Institute, an independent, multidisciplinary, nonprofit institution involved in social science research and the application of research findings to societal problems.

John Goodlad, (1990) professor of Education and director of the Center for Education Renewal at the University of Washington, Seattle.

Richard Paul (1985), director of the Center for Critical Thinking and Moral Critique at Sonoma State University, Rohnet Park, California.

David Perkins (1986), codirector of Harvard University's Project Zero, an interdisciplinary research project including the nature of cognitive abilities.

Michael Scrivan (1985), professor of Education at the University of Western Australia and former Alfred North Whitehead Fellow at Harvard University.

Robert Sternberg (1987), IBM Professor of Psychology and Education, Department of Psychology, Yale University.

This listing of reports and experts is by no means exhaustive. There is a growing volume of information regarding the benefits of direct teaching of thinking skills. The individuals selected are those whose works would be appropriate for any school executive or teacher to cite in support of a position for initiating a thinking skills program.

It seems that the only relatively new information in the "Nation at Risk" report is the call for technological literacy. But the document made headlines, and the droves of educators who had been crying for revisions in the "back-to-basics-rote-memory-out" to the "problem-solving-in" movement suddenly had a whole new audience: the ordinary person on the street. Articles appeared not only in journals designed for educators, but in household magazines and local newspapers. Cries for reform were heard in schools throughout North America.

School administrators and teachers, as a result of increased pressure not only from educational experts but also from parents, have become increasingly pressured to respond. Some schools have been fortunate enough to have the internal and external resources and support necessary to be among the first groups to initiate programs for improving thinking skills in the curriculum in order to meet the needs of an increasingly complex society. Some school districts have developed their own approaches, set up research studies, and now have data to support the continuance of these approaches. Others have adopted (and sometimes adapted) programs which were developed by outside experts. The decision as to whether adopting a packaged program or developing in-house training is the better method for teaching thinking skills must be made by the personnel in each school district, based on the specific needs of that district and using data regarding the effectiveness of any particular approach in similar situations.

In the area of thinking skills, strategies and methods for teaching both creative and critical thinking have been around for centuries. Much in theory and rationale but less in the area of hard data has been available regarding various approaches to the teaching of thinking skills. The most practical of the data available are presented in following chapters, along with some interpretive editorial comments.

A WORD ABOUT THE COMMON SENSE APPROACH

It is always appropriate to quote educational researchers who have scientifically designed (as much as possible with humans) research and prove as closely as possible that one or the other approach works for whatever deficient area in the curriculum. But how do you interpret the information so that it makes sense to the parent and student groups who are not up on Who's Who in educational research? Perhaps a few examples of the changes encountered by students in recent years will provide a pertinent analogy. Students now have ready access to hand calculators, videos and microcomputers. We are in a time of exploding information and technologies. The volume of information published yearly is staggering. How can we teachers of today possibly teach enough "facts" for the students of the next ten years? What will replace today's hand calculators, VCR's and microcomputer programs? Who will be creative enough and technical enough to invent the replacements? The very least we can teach our students now is how to weigh alternatives, think rationally, and to make reasonable decisions, not to conflict with the values taught at home, but to have the cognitive tools to rationally support them and to develop ideas. Then and only then will we be preparing students for the twenty-first century.[1]

ENDNOTES

1. "Knowing Is Not Thinking" by E. Janko, *Phi Delta Kappan*, March, 1989, pp. 543–544, and "Commentary, The 3 R's: Reading, Writing, and Reasoning" by J. Howard, April 22, 1987 *Education Week*, p. 23.

REFERENCES

APPLEBEE, A., J. Langer and I. Mullis. 1987. *Learning to Be Literate in America: Reading, Writing, and Reasoning*.

BENNETT, W. 1985. "First Lessons," *Education Week* (September).

BEREITER, C. 1984. "How to Keep Thinking Skills From Going the Way of All Frills," *Educational Leadership*, 42(1):75–77.

BOYER, E. 1985. "Critical Thoughts on Education," *National Forum*, 55(1):33–34.

DEWEY, J. 1910. *How We Think*. New York: D. D. Heath.

ENNIS, R. 1985. "Critical Thinking and the Curriculum," *National Forum*, 55(1):28–31.

GLASER, E. 1985. "Critical Thinking: Educating for Responsible Citizenship in a Democracy," *National Forum*, 55(1):24–27.

GOODLAD, J. 1990. "Better Teachers for Our Nation's Schools," *Phi Delta Kappan*, 72(3):185–194.

HENCHY, N. and D. Burgess. 1987. *Between Past and Future*. Calgary, Alberta: Detselig Enterprises Ltd.

National Commission on Excellence in Education. 1983. *A Nation At Risk: The Imperative for Educational Reform*. Washington, DC: The President's Council.

1983. *Academic Preparation for College*. New York: The College Board.

1983. *Education 2000*. B. Thwaites and C. Wysock-Wright, eds. Cambridge: Cambridge University Press.

PAUL, R. 1985. "The Critical Thinking Movement," *National Forum*, 55(1):2–3, 32.

PERKINS, D. 1986. "Thinking Frames," *Educational Leadership*, 43(8):4–11.

PERKINS, D. N. and H. Gardner. 1988. "Why 'Zero?' A Brief Introduction to Project Zero," *Journal of Aesthetic Education*, 22(1):viii–x.

Saskatchewan Education. 1988. *Common Essential Learnings* (Provincial Department of Education). Regina, Saskatchewan: Saskatchewan Education.

SCRIVEN, M. 1985. "Critical for Survival," *National Forum*, 55(1):9–12.

STERNBERG, R. 1987. *Teaching Thinking Skills*. New York: W. H. Freeman.

How to Choose a Thinking Skills Program

The major premise for teaching thinking skills is to better prepare students for life after school in a rapidly changing environment. Since we cannot possibly teach enough facts as used and accepted today and be confident that these facts will be used and accepted twenty, ten, or even five years from now, then we *must now* teach students how to determine in the future which facts are important for the situation. In other words, we *must* teach students how to think through problems and determine the best solution for a particular time and place. Teachers often respond to this premise by stating something to the effect that they already teach problem solving. To a certain extent, yes, but the evidence is overwhelming that such teaching (and learning) is not pervasive throughout the curriculum (see Chapter One for some of the research indicating this void).

So we agree that we do indeed need to do more in teaching students thinking skills. How do we do this? What do the "experts" recommend for teaching thinking skills? What are other schools doing that seems to be working? The answers are not worded as easily as the problem, as is typical in fields such as education where research deals with human beings with different personalities, different interests, different skill aptitudes, different levels of intelligence, and so on. As with any problem area in education, there are different approaches to solutions, depending on the point of view of the researcher, the nature of the student being researched, and the setting of the research. Some of the most thoroughly researched approaches are summarized in this book. And as with any current issue in education, research is being conducted daily on the programs discussed in this book, as well as on new programs. Most of the newest approaches have been left out of the discussion, not because of a lack of rationale to these approaches, but because less data are available as to their effectiveness.

APPROACHES TO TEACHING THINKING SKILLS

The paradigms, i.e., theoretical bases for the teaching of thinking skills, are quite technical in many regards. For purposes of simplicity, I am categorizing the programs as emphasizing (1) critical thinking, (2) creative thinking, or (3) the generic approach.

"Critical thinking" as defined by Sternberg (1986, p. 46) is "construed broadly, the mental processes, strategies, and representations people use to solve problems, make decisions, and learn new concepts."[2]

Ennis (1985, p. 45) has a slightly different wording: "Critical thinking is reflective and reasonable thinking that is focused on deciding what to believe or do." Ennis adds that there are creative aspects to critical thinking including "formulating hypothesis, questions, alternatives, and plans for experiments.[3] This creative aspect of Ennis's definition appears to correspond to the problem solving aspect of Sternberg's definition. Thus creative and critical thinking are treated as distinctly separate but complementary skills within the context of the approaches examined in this book.

"Creative thinking," as defined by Perkins (Brandt, 1986, p. 15), Brandt (1986, p. 15) "involves the generation and sifting of possibilities and reworking them."[4] In relating creativity and critical thinking Perkins also indicates that there are no clearly separated distinctions possible because "really good critical thinking . . . is insightful . . . and that, rather plainly, is creative thinking." However, it is obvious that different programs are strongly focused toward either creative or critical thinking to the extent that one can reasonably categorize the program as primarily one or the other.

The generic approach to teaching thinking skills involves both creative and critical thinking, not by use of a separate program but as theoretically infused throughout the curriculum. I say "theoretically" because of the lack of research regarding the effectiveness of this approach. The practicality of infusing thinking skills across the curriculum as the first and foremost approach is naive at best (and very possibly doomed to failure) because it actually requires the retraining of all teachers who have, in most cases, been very thoroughly trained already. This approach is criticized by many, including Perkins (in (Brandt, 1985, p. 17) and Sternberg (in Quinby, 1985, p. 51).

The most effective approach recommended (to paraphrase Sternberg, Perkins, and others) is to begin with a widely-researched program using a teacher (or two or ten) who is going to do a good job with the program as designed because s/he is voluntarily making the effort. A key component in selecting the program is whether it teaches the skills identified as needed by a particular school system, and the second very important factor is whether there is evidence of a transfer effect. That is, do the students who are participating in the thinking skills program show evidence of using the skills "learned" there in other subjects? If so, then you already have thinking skills achieved across the curriculum in a much more efficient manner than retraining all teachers skill by skill and subject by subject. Some of the thinking skills programs do have much evidence of bridging, i.e., transfer. The data in that regard are summarized in the following chapters, dealing with each program individually.

A simple analogy can by made with the skill of reading. Students obviously use reading skills in literature, science, social studies, mathematics, music, physical education, vocational education, etc., to varying degrees, depending on the activities. So should thinking skills, if the program is valid, be used by students in all subjects (to varying degrees). In the course of one's lifetime, reading materials change but the skill of reading remains. Facts which were read, understood and accepted as true years back are no longer pertinent, but the *skills* of reading and thinking remain valid skills. There will always be variations in individual reading proficiency, and there will be varying levels of proficiency in thinking skills. We are, after all, human beings and not robots. But evidence is strong that thinking skills can be taught and that the most efficient approach for initiating the teaching of thinking skills is to select a good program and add components as needed by each individual school.

TESTING

Schools test students to demonstrate (theoretically) that students are learning. Standardized tests are used to indicate a student's performance relative to other students of similar age and abilities across the country. U.S. schools use norms from U.S. schools, and Canadian schools use Canadian norms, although personal experience indicates that the curricula are very similar. Tests are used in virtually every North American school to indicate that students are either learning or not learning what they are supposed to within the curriculum.[5]

So how do you test whether or not students are learning better ways to think? The logical approach is twofold: (1) use a test designed specifically to test thinking skills (often called tests of reasoning) and (2) continue to use whatever standardized tests of achievement are now being used in your particular school system. A tentative design follows in the Evaluation section of a sample proposal presented at the end of this chapter.

A test of reasoning skills (see Appendix for specific listings) can be used with students before and after initiating a thinking skills program. If the students are performing better after the thinking skills program, then a safe conclusion to make is that they are learning some thinking skills as a result of that program. If students also perform better on standardized achievement tests, then a parallel conclusion can be made as to the transfer effect. (With apologies to statisticians, the testing issue is being consciously oversimplified for the sake of translating complex terminology into ordinary language.) If there are no staff members who are training in program evaluation, it is strongly recommended that an outside consultant be hired for at least a pilot project. College and university professors do such research as part of their professional role. You may also find a doctoral level graduate student who may be interested in conducting a study for minimal cost as part of a dissertation project. Colleges and universities also have resources to search out sources of funding for pilot and long-term studies. Many of the funding sources are available to schools only through such studies.

A SHORT COURSE IN PROPOSAL WRITING

A formal proposal for an outside source of funding (a grant) for a pilot project should contain several sections: Introduction, Rationale, Program Description, Objectives, Procedures, Personnel, Facilities, Time Frame, Evaluation, Budget. If the proposal is lengthy, include a Table of Contents. If the proposal is to a group within the school system, use the same sequence, but adjust the wording as necessary in terms of your audience. Specifically, the school board may want more details regarding budget adjustments, while a parent group may want more details as to the need for the program and how its effect(s) on students' academic performance will be measured. Again, for first-timers in proposal writing, a strong recommendation is to enlist outside help from a college or university. A simplified proposal follows.[6]

Introduction

The Introduction should contain some general statements regarding the purpose for the proposed project. One paragraph should include the significance in terms of timing, and another paragraph should be about the general feasibility of the whole program.

Rationale

The Rationale contains the specific reasons for initiating this project: (1) needs as identified/measured by school personnel and, (2) briefly, how the improvements anticipated will be of benefit to students. Make your case with a good degree of emotion—you are appealing to moms and dads to support changes in the curriculum which will make Susie and Johnnie better students and better citizens! On the other hand, keep in mind that the language must make sense to them in businesslike terms, otherwise you will have lost your case even before you have begun. A carefully prepared cost analysis, for example, will be a waste of time if your audience hasn't emotionally "bought in" to the idea at this point. Cite reports pertinent to the need for the direct teaching of thinking skills. Indicate specifically why this particular program seems right for your district—studies conducted using students with similar socioeconomic and ethnic backgrounds, for example.

Program Description

Thoroughly describe the program in terms of theoretical background and the way the program is packaged and presented. Tell if it is workbook format for students, if there are separate materials for teachers' reference, and if the materials are reusable. Samples can usually be obtained from the publisher or author.

Objectives

State how the rationale for this program fits into your school curriculum and what you expect to change as far as student achievement.

Procedures

Describe the teacher training involved in terms of how and when it is to be conducted. Describe how the program will then be implemented in the schools. Be specific as to the number of hours per week that students are expected to spend on the program in order for it to be effective.

Personnel

Identify who will train teachers, and which teachers and administrators are directly and indirectly involved in both the training and implementation of the program. Be sure to include whether or not a consultant will be necessary periodically throughout the implementation phase.

Facilities

Tell where the training will be conducted, where the program will be taught and where any other in-service activities regarding the program will be conducted.

Time Frame

Include teacher and administrator training and teaching, usually in terms of hours per week, with totals per semester or year. (Rarely is a thinking skills pilot program conducted for less than one semester. Two-year programs are quite common; there is no quick-fix to the teaching of thinking skills.)

Evaluation

A Possible Design

Intact-group comparison—rarely can school randomly assign students to control or experimental groups; the usual method is to compare classes within the same grade in schools with comparable social-ethnic mixes.

treatment:	yes	no
Intact Experimental Group	X	
Intact Control Group		X

Budget

(tentative)

Personnel	
Project Director—name	
25% of 9 months	$XX,000.00
Secretary—name	
10% of 9 months	$ X,000.00
Fringe Benefits	
(to include Social Security, hospitalization,	
unemployment compensation)	
17% of personnel costs	$ X,000.00
Consultant—name	
25% of 9 months base salary	$ X,000.00
Office Rental	
10 months	$ X,000.00
Supplies	
materials	$ X,000.00
TOTAL PROJECTED BUDGET	$XX,000.00

ENDNOTES

2. Robert Sternberg is a Yale psychologist who has written extensively about intelligence and thinking skills.

3. Robert Ennis is Director of the Illinois Critical Thinking Project and Professor of Philosophy, Department of Educational Policy Studies, University of Illinois at Urbana-Champaign.

4. David Perkins is Co-Director of Harvard University's Project Zero and author of extensive articles about creative and critical thinking.

5. A very thorough examination of the testing issue can be found in the October, 1985 issue of *Educational Leadership*. Sixteen articles present various aspects of the problems involved in schools testing of students.

6. For more details, two sources are recommended: *Guidelines for Preparing the Research Proposal* by J. H. Behling and *The Process of Grant Proposal Development*, Phi Delta Kappa Fastback #143. A more detailed source is *Making*

It Happen, Designing Research with Implementation in Mind by M. Hakel, et al.

REFERENCES

BEHLING, J. A. 1984. *Guidelines for Preparing the Research Proposal.* New York: University Press of America.

BRANDT, R. 1986. "On Creativity and Thinking Skills: A Conversation with David Perkins," *Educational Leadership*, 43(8):13–18.

ENNIS, R. 1985. "A Logical Basis for Measuring Critical Thinking Skills," *Educational Leadership*, 43(2):45–47.

HAKEL, M., M. Beer and J. Moses. 1982. *Making it Happen: Designing Research With Implementation in Mind.* Beverly Hills, CA: Sage.

QUINBY, N. 1985. "On Testing and Teaching Intelligence: A Conversation with Robert Sternberg," *Educational Leadership*, 43(2):50–53.

STERNBERG, R. 1986. *Intelligencer Applied.* New York: Harcourt Brace Jovanovich.

TEAGUE, G. and B. Heathington. 1980. *The Process of Grant Proposal Development.* Phi Delta Kappa Fastback #143. Bloomington, IN: Phi Delta Kappa Educational Foundation.

3

Philosophy for Children

OVERVIEW

The author of *Philosophy for Children*, Matthew Lipman, developed what has become one of the most widely used thinking skills programs as a result of personal dissatisfaction with the lack of such teaching in his own children's schooling.[7] Lipman contends that better thinking in the classroom primarily means better thinking in language; better thinking in language implies the need for teaching reasoning. In order to make reasoning processes meaningful to younger students, he developed materials which incorporate thinking skills of traditional philosophy but within the context of easily readable novels. In other words, rather than have students learn the complex terminology of college philosophy classes, philosophical issues are woven within the context of stories about students of about the same ages as students reading the novel-texts. Characters in the novels appear in situations which the reader can relate to both in and out of school.

The program is currently available in reading levels from approximately grade one through adult education.

The aim of the program, according to Lipman (ed. Costa, 1985, p. 212) "is to promote excellent thinking: thinking that is creative as well as critical, imaginative as well as logical, inventive as well as analytical."

Thinking skills which students in Philosophy for Children classrooms practice and coordinate (IAPC, 1987) include:

- analyzing value statements
- classifying and categorizing
- constructing hypotheses
- defining terms

- developing concepts
- discovering alternatives
- drawing inferences from hypothetical syllogisms
- drawing inferences from single premises
- drawing inferences from double premises
- finding underlying assumptions
- formulating causal explanations
- formulating comparisons as relationships
- formulating questions
- generalizing
- giving reasons
- grasping part-whole and whole-part connections
- identifying and using criteria
- knowing how to deal with ambiguities
- knowing how to treat vagueness
- looking out for informal fallacies
- making connections
- making distinctions
- predicting consequences
- providing instances and illustrations
- recognizing contextual aspects of truth and falsity
- recognizing differences of perspective
- recognizing interdependence of means and ends
- seriation
- standardizing ordinary language sentences
- taking all considerations into account
- using ordinal or relational logic
- working with analogies
- working with consistency and contradiction

RATIONALE

Lipman advocates that thinking skills should be taught in the context of a humanistic discipline, so as to guard against the skills being misused. The most appropriate discipline in the humanities for teaching critical thinking, according to Lipman, is philosophy. The title of the first novel written, *Harry Stottlemeier's Discovery*, is a pun on the name Aristotle. Lipman suggests that the process whereby the early Greeks developed philosophy in the search for perfection of the thinking process is similar to the process whereby children today develop thinking skills. Lipman's Aristotelian novel is written at reading/thinking level skills suitable for grades 5–8.

The K–12 integration of philosophical thinking is necessary in today's curriculum because (Lipman, 1985, p. 3) "philosophy is the discipline that best prepares us to think in terms of the other disciplines. . . ." This preparation is what psychologists refer to as transfer, or bridging. To the layman, that means simply that there is a carryover effect with skills learned in one area that helps students to better understand and perform in other areas of the curriculum. According to Lipman (1980, p. 11) ". . . education, both from the child's point of view and from the parents', should be imbued with thoughtfulness and reasonableness . . . An education that . . . promises to be an academically superior education, in measurable terms, and even more valuable as an instrument for beyond-school experience."

That transfer is built into Philosophy for Children is also a conclusion that Sternberg and Bhana (1986, p. 64) support in a detailed technical analysis of various thinking skills programs.

An extremely important component of the program is that students should not be just *exhorted* to be proud of themselves but helped to *develop* competencies that they themselves recognize as individual accomplishments. In regard to the economically disadvantaged, Lipman concludes that this is all the more important because "they have few other resources to call upon in life than their wits. . . ." (1985, p. 11).[8]

The program places much emphasis on class discussion. Students read small portions of their text, i.e., novel, then raise questions for discussion among the group, a process Lipman calls developing a "community of inquiry." The teacher acts as a monitor for the discussion and writes the questions raised for discussion on the chalkboard. The students' names are also written by their questions on the chalkboard. A sense of self-esteem develops in students in noting this seemingly simple, but very important aspect of recognition of the worth of the student's thoughts. (In no classroom other than in those doing Philosophy for Children have I personally observed this technique being used.) When students see their questions publically displayed, a sense of validation is apparent in their attitudes. Many classroom teachers note this attitude as a positive aspect affecting general class management as a result of the program.

Teachers often express surprise at the enthusiasm of students for this type of philosophical discussion. "A calm discussion period it is not, with hands waving, bodies bouncing, faces reddening. Amazingly they are listening to each other" (Brent, in Chance, 1986, p. 55). Teachers also report of students raising philosophical questions in other classes, including math and history (typically classes involving much rote memorization of facts).

A surprising aspect of the program is the carryover effect out of the classroom. Reed and Henderson (reported in Chance, p. 56), found that 80 percent of the students who had participated in Philosophy for Children in their study said that they talked about their philosophy classes with their parents or other adults. Any parent who has gone through the "What did you learn in school today? Nothing," routine can appreciate this report!

At least one parent has reported dramatic behavioral changes in a student after the student participated for several weeks in Philosophy for Children (Hamrick, 1987). The child had withdrawn into a shell, not talking at home or in other classes at school. When the mother attended a class demonstration of the program, she was astounded to observe her child discussing as enthusiastically as the other students in class.

Mulvaney (1986, p. 2) describes the program as stressing self-discovery in a way that few, if any, of the elements of the "regular curriculum" can claim to do. This deference to the self-definition and self-esteem of the student, according to Mulvaney, "makes every child a winner."

A BRIEF HISTORY OF THE PROGRAM

The Institute for the Advancement of Philosophy for Children (IAPC) originated in 1969 and has been expanding steadily since 1974 (Lipman et al., 1980, p. 51).

In addition to the U.S. and Canada, the program has been used in the United Kingdom, Australia, New Zealand, France, Taiwan, Israel, Spain, Mexico, Ecuador, Chile, Guatemala, Germany, Holland, Austria, Portugal, Denmark, Egypt, and Iceland (Bulletin, 1989).

A resolution was raised in the European Parliament in December, 1987, calling for financial support and encouragement to the development of primary school philosophy in all member nations (Lipman, 1988, p. 16).

In 1986, the program was labeled "meritorious" by the National Diffusion Network, a branch of the U.S. Department of Education (Shea, 1987, p. 1).

DESCRIPTION OF MATERIALS

K-2 Target Grade Range

The first text/novel, *Elfie*, is appropriate for students with reading abilities of approximately 1.2 (the second half of a typical grade one). The theme is reasoning about thinking (psychologists refer to this as metacognition). Thinking skills/concepts covered in *Elfie* include:

- the differences between appearance and reality
- the one and the many
- parts and wholes
- similarity and difference
- permanence and change
- change and growth

The teacher's manual is entitled *Getting Our Thoughts Together*. It contains exercises designed to aid students in dialogue and also provides opportunities to aid students into organizing their experiences into verbalized story form as a prerequisite for learning to write. The term "opportunity" is used because the amount of examples provided is about three times more than can be used in one year. The teacher selects those exercises which support the thinking skills that students have raised in their discussions.

2–3 Target Grades

The student's novel is *Kio and Gus*. The book is considered an introduction to science and environmental education in covering concepts of

- make-believe and reality
- fear and courage
- saying and doing
- truth and beauty

Wondering at the World, the teachers manual, provides a choice of hundreds of discussion plans and exercises which can be used to assist the development of cognitive skills by which we understand nature.

3–4 Target Grades

Pixie is written in larger than usual type for this age group, in order to assist less able readers. The text is designed as an introduction to inquiry skills which are necessary for understanding the next novel-text in the series, *Harry Stottlemeier's Discovery*. The reading level is approximately grade 4. *Pixie* includes inquiry skills which purport to help students in:

- developing class and family relationships
- understanding rules, reasons and excuses
- logical, social, familiar, aesthetic, causal,
- part-whole, mathematical concepts
- ratios, similes, metaphors and analogies

The teacher's manual, *Looking for Meaning*, contains 390 pages of choices of activities and reasoning skill exercises to assist the teacher in enhancing students understanding. The emphasis is on the development of the inquiry skills of generalization, classification, concept development, making comparisons, offering counterexamples, using analogies, contradiction and seriation.

5–6 Target Grades

Harry Stottlemeier's Discovery provides the techniques of critical thinking which students in later grades are expected to use in more specific problems in science, social studies, and language arts. The text offers a model of dialogue of children with each other and with adults. The novel encourages the development of alternative modes of thought and imagination:

- how children might learn profitably from one another
- that children are capable at times of engaging in their own cooperative inquiry for no other reason that the satisfaction of doing so

This text is also used in grades 7–8 if the students have not studied *Pixie*.

The teacher's manual, *Philosophical Inquiry*, was first published in 1978 and was thoroughly revised in 1984. The revision incorporated recommendations made from teachers who had thoroughly field-tested the program. The teacher's manual contains discussion plans, exercises and activities which operationalize several aspects of inquiry as to differences of kind and degree. In other words, it is designed to refine and hone thinking skills which were introduced in *Pixie*.

There are guidelines and questions with suggestions for the teacher. In addition, each chapter concludes with a section devoted to teacher self-evaluation (as opposed to student-evaluation).[9]

A version of this text called *Harry Prime* has been developed for adult literacy programs at the request of the Office of Adult Literacy in Washington, D. C. This version has been used in Quebec and Brazil as well as the U.S. (Center for Analytic Teaching, 1988, p. 7).

7–8 Target Grades

Lisa is a sequel to *Harry*, with most of the same characters as earlier novels but focusing on older brothers, sisters, friends. The goal is to provide students with the tools of inquiry so that they can become more thoughtful, considerate and reasonable beings. The novel is designed to provide the basic concepts of ethical inquiry:

- good, right, fair
- consistency, truth, logical relationships
- rules and criteria
- circumstances

The teacher's manual is called *Ethical Inquiry*. It is currently in its second edition. The classroom dialogue to accompany *Lisa* is to be regulated by the teacher through the structuring of exercises and discussion plans so as to be assured that the aspects of the thinking skills are being dealt with thoroughly. Topics include:

- gift-giving
- lying
- stealing
- cruelty
- atonement

with discussion plans including:

- appealing to consistency, to consequences, to good reasons
- the reason/cause distinction
- universalization
- taking contextual circumstances into account
- categorical and conditional syllogisms

9–10 Target Grades

Suki is designed for reasoning in language arts. The central character is a girl named Suki, who wrestles with the obstacles that students of her age often encounter in trying to write poetry and fiction.

The teacher's manual is titled *Writing: How and Why*. It contains an anthology of hundreds of poems by and for children and young adults. There are also many choices of exercises, including conversational modes.

11–12 Target Grades

Mark is designed for reasoning in social studies. Mark and his classmates discuss such issues as

- crime and society
- being a victim of society
- what forces hold society together or work to pull it apart
- social institutions
- rules and values
- tradition
- bureaucracy
- authority
- responsibility
- force
- democracy, freedom and justice

The teacher's manual is called *Social Inquiry*. The goal is to focus students' already developed thinking skills upon the conceptual foundations, i.e., the root issues of the social sciences.[10]

RESEARCH REGARDING EFFECTIVENESS

The National Diffusion Network of the United States Department of Education endorsed the program as being "meritorious" only after approximately ten years of program use and validated testing of over 5,000 students in 10 schools (Shea, 1987, 1). Approximately 5,000 school districts (including public, private and parochial) in North America are using the program (Brandt, September, 1988, p. 35).

Periodically, research results are reported in *Thinking*, the journal of philosophy for children.

More research to date has been conducted with middle grades; however, there are also some positive results from some K–12 studies. The "New Jersey Test of Reasoning" is the test of thinking skills most often used (both English and French versions exist). Various standardized achievement test results have also been positively affected by students participating in the program, including the California Achievement Test, Reasoning on Analogies (Ontario Institute for Studies in Education), Torrance Test of Creative Thinking (fluidity, flexibility, originality), the Metropolitan Achievement Test, and the California Test of Mental Maturity. Gains in reading comprehension as well as in mathematics performance have been attributed to students participation in the program.

Most studies are of students within what is typically called mainstream classrooms, although there have been several positive studies reported with special populations (with various modifications to the program), including deaf, gifted, low-achievers (including every major ethnic category), ESL students, learning-disabled, and emotionally handicapped children.

Studies indicating gender differences demonstrated in testing either have not been conducted or results have indicated no differences.

Several anecdotal reports include positive comments in subjective (affective) comments by teachers, students and parents.

Several studies are reported (1984, IAPC) in this regard: Curtis (1979), reports that 82 percent of the 300 fifth- and sixth-grade students studied said they would like to take another philosophy course, and 92 percent said they would recommend it to their friends. Cinquino (1980) found that 33 of 35 parents interviewed wanted their children to continue participating in the program.

IMPLEMENTATION PROCEDURES

Teacher Training

There are several options of in-service training programs available from the IAPC. All involve consultants from the IAPC, but the blocks of time spent with teachers vary. The initial training recommended for teachers is approximately two weeks. In addition, periodic visits during the year by an IAPC-trained consultant are scheduled. (The consultants have PhDs in Philosophy or EdDs in Philosophy of Education with additional training in Philosophy for Children from the IAPC.) The format of the teacher-training includes teachers participating in the program as students, i.e., modeling the format that is to be used in their classrooms. Teachers thus practice the thinking skills in the program and discuss pedagogical questions about the program (Philosophy for Children Information Pamphlet, 1987, S16).

The program does not teach thinking skills as separate "technical" skills. That is, the awareness of logical rules are not taught as enough to make a person a better thinker. Other requirements identified as necessary include good will, imagination, and an appreciation of other people's points of views.

Teacher-proof? Definitely not. Lipman (1988, p. 37) describes the program as requiring a "special kind of teacher . . . who inspires trust, so that there's openness in the classroom, a teacher who is thoughtful and reflective . . . ." In other words, the type of questioning that a teacher uses is very inportant, so that students are able to express themselves clearly and openly. The teaching style required (to summarize) is dialectic (involving discussion), rather than didactic (teacher directed) (Mayes, 1988, p. 8).

Training may also be available through the Maryland Center for Thinking Studies at Coppin State College. The Center was established in July 1988 and when fully operational will include a unit for training teachers and teacher trainers in Philosophy for Children. This Center puts special emphasis on the training of college and university faculty in historically Black colleges and universities.

Time Required of Students

The recommended participation time for students in the program is approximately 160 minutes per week. Teachers in lower grades spend 30–45 minutes per session; upper grades spend up to 60 minutes per session (IAPC, 1987). The time slots usually fall into blocks allotted to language arts or social studies.

Costs

Teacher's manuals are approximately $40.00 (U.S.) each, but are reusable for several years. They consist of huge 3-ring notebooks with pages easily removable for duplication of exercises. Student texts cost about $8.00 each, but as soft covers, are reusable two or three years on the average, depending on the handling. Students do not take the novels home, so they remain stored in classrooms other than when the actual reading-discussion takes place. The IAPC estimates a cost per pupil of $21.50 to $33.00 during the first year (depending upon the method of teacher training), and about $2.70 per pupil for ensuing years.

ENDNOTES

7. Personal communication, October, 1986.

8. For a thorough explanation of the program, see *Philosophy in the Classroom* by Matthew Lipman, Ann Margaret Sharp, and Frederick S. Oscanyan.

9. The students are not supposed to be formally graded on their performance/participation in the program. Lipman contends that this would lead to a teacher-centered discussion, which is contrary to the essence of developing of improved student thinking. I have not encountered teachers who find this lack of grading a problem, once they get students trained in the discussion format of the program.

10. More detailed descriptions of the materials and training options are available by writing to the Institute for the Advancement of Philosophy for Children, Montclair State College, Upper Montclair, NJ 07043. There are also several other books, two newsletters (one for the U.S. and one international), and a scholarly-type yet readable journal about the program available from the IAPC.

REFERENCES

Abeil Foundation & U.S. Department of Education. January, 1989. *The Maryland Center for Thinking Studies*, Washington, DC (Eric Document # ED 306 879).

BRANDT, R. 1988. "On Philosophy in the Curriculum: A Conversation with Matthew Lipman," *Educational Leadership*. 46(1):34–37.

Center for Analytic Teaching, ed. 1988. *The Philosophy for Children Newsletter*, Institute Notes. 3(3).

CHANCE, P. 1986. *Thinking in the Classroom*. A Survey of Programs. New York: Teachers College Press.

COSTA, A., ed. 1985. *Developing Minds. A Resource Book for Teaching Thinking*. Alexandria, VA: Association for Supervision and Curriculum Development.

HAMRICK, W. S. 1987. "A Real-Life Brian," *Thinking, 7.* "The Journal of Philosophy for Children."

Institute for the Advancement of Philosophy for Children. 1984. *Bulletin Supplement*. Upper Montclair, NJ: IAPC.

International Council for Philosophical Inquiry with Children. 1989. *Bulletin, 3.*

LIPMAN, M. 1985. *Philosophical Practice and Educational Reform.* Washington, DC: (Eric Document # ED 269 973).

LIPMAN, M. 1988. "A Motion Under Discussion in the European Parliament with Regard to Philosophy for Children," *Thinking.* 7(4):16–17.

LIPMAN, M., Sharp, A. M. and F. S. Oscanyan. 1980. *Philosophy in the Classroom.* Philadelphia: Temple University Press.

MAYES, W. 1988. "Thinking Skills Programs: An Analysis," *Thinking,* 7(4):2–11.

MULVANEY, R. J. 1986. "Philosophy for Children in Its Historical Context," *Thinking,* 6(2):2–8.

Philosophy for Children Information Pamphlet. 1987. Upper Montclair, NJ: Institute for the Advancement of Philosophy for Children.

SHEA, P. 1987. *The Philosophy for Children Newsletter,* 2(2):1.

STERNBERG, R. and K. Bhana. 1986. "Synthesis of Research on the Effectiveness of Intellectual Skills Programs: Snake-Oil Remedies or Miracle Cures?" *Educational Leadership,* 44(2):60–67.

4

Instrumental Enrichment

OVERVIEW

The author of Instrumental Enrichment is Reuven Feuerstein. Instrumental Enrichment is frequently shortened in references to FIE or IE. The goal of the program is to develop thinking skills (problem-solving abilities) in order for students to become active, self-motivated and independent thinkers. The assumption underlying this goal is that intelligence is modifiable, i.e., subject to upward changes. This assumption means that teachers can provide direct intervention and mediated (controlled) learning experiences which result in improved student performance in thinking.

It is important to be aware of terms. Feuerstein refers to the student whose performance needs changes as the "retarded performer" in a manner that is consistent with the term "underachiever" as typically used by classroom teachers in North America. Although FIE was piloted in a research study with students who were categorized as "Educably Mentally Retarded," the program has since been used with students who may actually be capable of performance in the gifted range, but who are performing very poorly in school. Thus those educators/parents who may have read some of Feuerstein's book or articles are cautioned not to be "put off" the program by thinking that it is applicable only to students in special education programs (see the research summary at the end of the chapter). Remember that the "retarded performer" label is used in a very technical sense in FIE; an underlying assumption is that the student is quite capable of much better performance, given proper instruction. FIE purports to provide that instruction to all but the most severely retarded performers.

Retarded performance, in this sense, is a temporary state. Retarded performers characteristically do not make connections based on former experiences. They do not build relationships. They view the world and learning in an episodic, sporadic manner. These characteristics are demonstrated both in and out of school.

Content-Free Approach

FIE purports to provide students with tools for learning to learn (Link, 1985, p. 94). As much as possible, Instrumental Enrichment avoids the use of content, meaning that it is to be taught at times separate from the label of any other subject. The reasoning for this approach, briefly, is to better hold the attention of the student on the skills, rather than confuse him/her with the additional burden of trying to remember facts as well. The teacher is then able to focus the child on the goal of the tasks. The content of any instrument if considered only a vehicle which is secondary to the major goal: the acquisition of thinking skills (Feuerstein et al., 1980, p. 119).

Since this program is designed for students who have already had several years of experience and frustration with mastering content, the theory is that the student is more motivated when practicing the thinking skills of this program as a new, separate and interesting aspect of school. Once the student experiences success in FIE, s/he can then be encouraged to make subject-matter content more meaningful by using the FIE strategies in mastering that content. In this approach, the teacher obviously is an essential element in assisting/reminding the student to transfer these skills.

Link (1985, p. 90) has summarized six major goals of Instrumental Enrichment:

(1) To correct deficiencies in cognitive functions
(2) To help students to learn and apply the basic operations of effective thinking
(3) To produce sound and spontaneous thinking habits leading to greater self-confidence and motivation
(4) To produce in students increasingly reflective and insightful thinking
(5) To motivate students toward task-oriented abstract goals rather than toward impulsive self-gratification
(6) To transform poor learners from the role of passive recipients into active generators of new information

There are elements of creative thinking in the goals of FIE, notably in the goals of (1) insightful student thinking and (2) in generating new information.

The Cognitive Functions of Instrumental Enrichment include:

Gathering information (input)

(1) Using senses to gather information
(2) Using a system or plan
(3) Labeling the information gathered
(4) Describing things and events in terms of where and when they occur
(5) Deciding on the characteristics of constancy
(6) Organizing information by using more than one source of information
(7) Being precise and accurate

Using information (elaboration)

(1) Defining the problem
(2) Using (of the information gathered) relevant data
(3) Having a picture in mind of what must be done
(4) Making a step-by-step plan of action
(5) Remembering the information needed for solving the problem
(6) Looking for relationships
(7) Comparing objects and experiences in terms of similarities and differences
(8) Categorizing the new object or experience
(9) Thinking about different possibilities and consequences
(10) Using logic to defend opinions

Expressing the solution to a problem (output)

(1) Being clear and precise in language
(2) Thinking things through before answering
(3) Restraining impulsive behavior

(4) Not panicking if a question cannot be immediately answered, even though the answer is "known"

Rationale

Feuerstein developed the program on a conception of intelligence that emphasizes processes rather than mere recollection of facts. He was dissatisfied with conventional intelligence testing as not measuring students' abilities to process information. Feuerstein has conducted more than 20 years of research in supporting his belief about intelligence. He strongly opposes the theory that intelligence is primarily an inborn ability. Rather, he states that ". . . intelligence is considered a dynamic self-regulation process that is responsive to external environmental intervention" (Feuerstein Rand, Hoffman, and Miller, 1980, p. 2). That process of changing intelligence, is called cognitive modifiability (Feuerstein et al., 1980, p. 9). The student's poor performance is due to a lack of Mediated Learning Experiences (MLE), according to Feuerstein (1980, p. 13). A discussion of the lack of MLE in terms of cultural deprivation gets quite technical. Feuerstein has a very specific definition of culture as "the process by which knowledge, values, and beliefs are transmitted from one generation to the next" (1980, p. 13). In this definition, cultural deprivation is the result of a failure on the part of a group to transmit (i.e., mediate) its culture to its children.

Feuerstein's discussion of MLE is quite lengthy, including his theory on the emotional attachment necessary between a mother and child. The summary presented here is at best a brief paraphrasing of a very thoroughly detailed rationale as to his program.

It seems important to note that although the program is now being used in many "normal" classrooms, Feuerstein seems to be unenthusiastic about this generalization of the program (as reported in Chance, p. 81). To paraphrase, the program is described as not being wasted upon average or above-average students, as long as the diagnostic element remains. That is, as long as specific deficiencies are diagnosed in the students. The North American coordinator of FIE, Frances Link, is enthusiastic about the use of FIE in regular classrooms; however, for districts with limited funding, the recommendation remains (if a choice has to be made) to use FIE with the underachievers (F. Link, personal communication, May 18, 1989).

A BRIEF HISTORY OF THE PROGRAM

FIE (Feuerstein's Instrumental Enrichment) relies heavily on a diagnostic method called the (LPAD) Learning Potential Assessment Device (Feuerstein et al., p. xix). The work on the LPAD began around 1955 in Israel, partially inspired by the work of Piaget. The original students of interest were immigrant adolescents in Israel whose low scores on intelligence testing and poor school performance indicated a gap in their level of cognitive functioning ranging between three and six years behind their peers. Twenty-one such cognitive deficiencies have been identified by Feuerstein. Conventional IQ tests did not provide a diagnosis for these students in terms of potential, but only provided a report of low scores in comparison to peers. The LPAD was designed to fill this gap. Feuerstein rejected the notion by some that IQ test scores by the students in question were fixed and therefore schools could do little or nothing with these students.

The LPAD identifies the student's learning and reasoning abilities in terms of (1) the capacity to grasp the principle underlying an initial problem, (2) the amount and type of instruction required to teach the student the given principle, (3) the extent to which the newly acquired principle is successfully applied, (4) the student's preference(s) for alternative methods of presentation of a problem, and (5) the effects of different training strategies offered in the remediation of the student's functioning (R. Sternberg, 1985, p. 234).

Expansion to North America

Feuerstein credits Professor H. Carl Haywood as playing a key role in the development and coordination of research on Instrumental Enrichment conducted in North America. Haywood and others have established a center for research at Vanderbilt University in Nashville, Tennessee. He coordinated research with others at the Ontario Institute for Studies in Education in Toronto. A continuing research project on FIE since 1970 is the Hadassah-Wizo-Canada Research Institute (Feuerstein, et. al., 1980, p. xxii). FIE is now part of the standard curriculum for approximately 30,000 Israeli students.

Frances Link of Curriculum Development Associates in Washington, D.C., has been instrumental in the implementation of FIE in the United States. An ongoing evaluation project involving Nashville, Louisville,

New York, Phoenix, and Toronto was undertaken in 1977 (Nickerson, Perkins, and Smith, 1985, Chapter 6). Several positive results have been reported. (See the research summary at the end of the chapter for more details.) The program has been used and formally evaluated at the Calgary Learning Center (Conte, 1983).

In 1986, Link (Savell, p. 381) reported approximately 800 school districts in 40 states as using the program. School populations ranged from city-core, to multi-ethnic, to rural. And in addition, the U.S. army has explored the program in regard to teaching leadership-relevant thinking skills to prospective army leaders (J. M. Savell, 1986). The program is also being piloted in Venezuela.

DESCRIPTION OF MATERIALS

The Feuerstein Instrumental Enrichment program consists of more than 500 pages of paper-and-pencil exercises. These exercises are divided into 15 modules which Feuerstein calls instruments. Each of the instruments addresses a specific cognitive (thinking skill) deficiency. FIE exercises can be grouped into two broad categories: (1) those that are appropriate for even the functionally illiterate, and (2) those that require a "relatively proficient" level of reading and verbal comprehension. The program is used typically with upper elementary through secondary students (ages 11–adult) as a supplement to the regular curriculum (Feuerstein, Rand, Hoffman, and Miller, 1980, Chapter 7).

Non-Verbal Instruments

Organization of Dots. The student's task is to identify and outline, within these sets of dots, sets of geometric figures such as squares, triangles, diamonds, and stars. This appears to be a device for bridging perceptual differences similar to those identified by some psychologists.[11]

Analytic Perception. The student's task is to identify shapes within larger shapes.

Illustrations. The student is shown a series of pictures illustrating an absurdity; the student must say why the sequence is absurd.

Those instruments that have a limited vocabulary (specific reading level not given) include:

Orientation in Space I and III. The student has tasks to illustrate understanding of concepts of left, right, front, back, and point of view.

Comparisons. One example: the student is to indicate which attributes of direction, number, color, form, and size differ from their presentation in comparison pictures.

Family Relations. The student is asked to respond to questions such as "What are there more of in the world: sons or fathers? Why?"

Numerical Progressions. Tasks include geometric (shapes) and numerical series continuations.

Syllogisms. The student is presented with a variety of verbal and pictorial syllogisms to solve (deductive reasoning).

Those instruments requiring independent reading and comprehension skills of typical adolescents include:

Categorization. One example involves the student in identifying pictures of common objects, then grouping those objects into categories (such as objects that give light, objects that are means of transportation, and the like).

Instructions. The student must understand and follow sets of instructions.

Temporal Relations. The student must explain events such as why one student arrived home half an hour later than another student when they both left school on their bikes at the same time and traveled at the same speed.

Transitive Relations. The student must solve tasks such as: if A is greater than B, and B is greater than C, what is the relation between A and C?

Representational Stencil Designs. The student must construct a design that is identical to that in a colored standard.

Instruments typically used in the first year of a three-year program include (Link, 1985, p. 95) Organization of Dots, Orientation in Space I, Comparisons, and Analytic Perception. Second year instruments include Categorization, Instructions, Temporal Relations, Numerical Progressions, Family Relationships, and Illustrations. The instruments typically used in the third year are Transitive Relations and Syllogisms, Representational Stencil Design, and Orientation in Space III.

Several other instruments in various stages of development (Feuerstein, 1980, p. 126) include Absurdities, Analogies, Convergent and

Divergent Thinking, Illusions, Language and Symbolic Comprehension, Maps, and Auditory and Haptic Discrimination.[12]

Except for Illustrations and Temporal Relations, exercises in each instrument are graduated in levels of difficulty, dependent on mastery of the earlier instruments. Each instrument has its own cover and is subdivided into units of a size which would typically be called sections rather than units by most North American teachers.

RESEARCH REGARDING EFFECTIVENESS

A two-year pilot study of FIE in the United States involved hearing-impaired adolescents in Washington, D.C. (Martin, in Link, 1985, p. 99). Experimental group students (those receiving FIE training) and control group students (those not receiving FIE) groups were compared in regard to general cognitive functioning, problem-solving strategies, and reading comprehension. Students in clinical settings trained in FIE demonstrated improvements indicating positive results in thinking skills attributable to participating in the program. The enthusiasm of teachers in the pilot reportedly led to the involvement of several additional teachers in the program for ensuing years. Gallaudet University in Washington, D.C., has become a center for training teachers of hearing impaired in the U.S. by conducting summer institutes under the direction of Dean David Martin (Link, 1990).

A 1980–81 study in New York City, as reported by Link (1980, p. 101) involved non-public school, Chapter One students. The gains in quantitative and non-verbal performance as measured by the California Achievement Test (reading comprehension) and in total mathematics score on the Standard Achievement Test were significantly greater after training in FIE. In addition, individual enthusiasm for the program on the part of students and teachers was reported. One aspect of this enthusiasm was the support that teachers continually received from the program's administrators. Another aspect, reported anecdotally (verbally, not statistically), was the motivation that the program provided for students. Teachers described this as partially due to the fact that students had the chance to state their opinions, right or wrong. This helped them to get over the fear of making mistakes. (This aspect of students' verbalization of opinions is also an aspect that seems to increase students' motivation in school as in Philosophy for Children, although the two programs are very different in their overall design.)

A third report of the success of FIE is that teachers begin to expect more from students, a psychological phenomenon that has been researched in other classroom settings by Rosenthal and colleagues, called at various times the Rosenthal effect or the Pygmalion effect.

Other students reported by Link indicate positive gains in reading comprehension and in mathematics computation as a result of training in FIE.

Some important conclusions to the research are that (1) college is not too late in the modifications of cognitive functioning, (2) in-depth teacher training is an essential prerequisite to the success of the program, and (3) significant positive differences in achievement and overall self-confidence can be attributed to the program.

FIE has also been used, with positive results reported, in approximately twenty schools in the United Kingdom in both special schools and in comprehensive high schools with a wide variety of ages and populations. Most of the students in the U.K. study are described as "retarded performers," and some had behavior problems. Teachers additionally reported some improvements in attendance and noted some increases in pupils' attention spans.

A 1985 study in Schaumburg, Illinois, involved 428 fifth- and sixth-grade students. The Cognitive Abilities Test was used for pre-test and post-test comparisons (Link, 1985, p. 105). Quantitative and non-verbal subtest scores of the experimental group students were significantly higher than those of control group students. This increase was attributed to FIE training.

Feuerstein gives anecdotal examples of those benefiting from FIE over the years, including a college professor who at the age of fifteen had been functionally illiterate, and a student who had an IQ of 55 but after five and a half years of FIE was making Bs and Cs as a university student (Chance, p. 71).

A study conducted by Dufner and Alexander (1987) involved gifted fourth-grade students' performance on well-structured and ill-structured problems. Students trained in FIE consistently produced better quality responses, but students trained in a different thinking skills program (Future Problem Solving) were more fluent. The standardized tests used for assessing students' skills were the Standard Progressive Matrices and Exercises in Divergent Thinking.

Standardized tests which have been used to assess the program's transfer effect include portions of the Lorge-Thorndike Intelligence Test, Raven's Standard Progressive Matrices, some subtests of

Thurstone's Primary Mental Abilities Test, the Peabody Individual Achievement Test, and KeyMath Diagnostic Arithmetic Test, and the Wide-Range Achievement Test (Nickerson, Perkins, and Smith, 1985, p. 158).

Other tests which indicate positive gains in students' attitudes as a result of FIE are identified by Nickerson, Perkins, and Smith (1985) as the Intellectual Achievement Responsibility Questionnaire, the Rosenberg Self-Esteem Scale, the Piers-Harris Self-Concept Scale, the Picture Motivation Scale, Nowicki-Strickland Locus of Control Scale, and the Student's Environmental Preference Survey.

IMPLEMENTATION PROCEDURES

Teacher Training

The program is highly teacher-sensitive. The quality of interactions between teachers and students is described as more important than the program exercises themselves (Chance, 1986, p. 81).

Teacher training initially involves a minimum of 45 hours each year. The program is designed for a three year implementation schedule but can be adjusted to a two-year program. Training programs, as much as possible, are custom designed to fit individual school systems.

Training is divided into three areas:

(1) Understanding and accepting the fundamental theories and concepts of FIE

(2) Mastery in classroom planning and use of the instruments

(3) Special techniques for mediating, bridging, and applying cognitive processes to specific subject matter and to life experiences.

Teachers are described as playing a crucial role as the mediating agents of the program (Link, 1985, p. 98). The teacher, as the human element of the Mediated Learning Experience, learns how to apply elements of the program such as

- intentionality of meaning
- transcendence
- mediation of meaning
- mediation of feeling of competence
- mediated sharing behavior
- mediated regulation and control of behavior
- mediated individuation and psychological differentiation

- mediation of goal seeking, goal setting, and goal planning
- mediation of challenge, i.e., the search for novelty and complexity

An important aspect of the program is that a student's errors are viewed as a very important means to provide insights into how the student solves problems (R. Sternberg, 1985, p. 232). That is, errors are not merely marked as wrong and left at that.

Time Required of Students

Fourteen of the instruments are to be regularly used in any classroom implementation of the program through one-hour lessons, three to five days per week for two to three years.

For particular needs of individual students, i.e., prescriptive purposes, a psychologist, counselor, and/or teacher selects those instruments whose emphases match the specific needs of that individual pupil.

Costs

Options for the U.S. and Canada include a half-day (four hours minimum) introductory session (called Awareness Sessions for Decision-Making Purposes) which gives an overview of the curriculum and provides samples of materials used in the course.

For those districts planning to implement the program fully, five-day training sessions (called Implementation Planning) are available in three levels of increasing complexity.

Cost of first year implementation materials (four instruments):
    approximately $40 per teacher
    $325 per twenty students, $175 for ten students

Second year (six instruments):
    $50 per teacher's guide
    $350 for twenty students, $185 for ten students

Third year (four instruments):
    $55 per teacher's guide
    $400 for twenty students, $210 for ten students

Five days of training (costs comparable to other programs) are required for implementing each course of FIE. Training sessions are custom designed for each school district (Link, 1990).

ENDNOTES

11. This perceptual measure as identified by Witkin is called field-dependence/independence and is measured by the "Group Embedded Figures Test." A readable summary of this research is included in *Marching to Different Drummers* by Pat Burke Guild and Stephen Garger, published by ASCD (1985).

12. Descriptions of the programs are only briefly summarized here. For more information contact Dr. Frances R. Link, Curriculum Development Associates, Inc., Suite 414, 1211 Connecticut Avenue, NW, Washington, DC 20036.

REFERENCES

CHIPMAN, S. F., J. W. Segal and R. Glaser, eds. 1985. *Thinking and Learning Skills: Research and Open Questions. Volume 2.* Hillsdale, NJ: Lawrence Erlbaum.

CONTE, R. 1983. *The Evaluation of the Calgary Learning Centre, Summary.* ERIC Document Reproduction Services # ED246576. Calgary, Alberta: Calgary Society for Students with Learning Difficulties.

DUFNER, H. A. and P. A. Alexander. 1987. *Effects of Training in Problem Solving on the Problem-Solving Abilities of Gifted Fourth Graders: A Comparison of the Future Problem Solving and Instrumental Enrichment Programs.* ERIC Document Reproduction Services # ED282934.

EMERSON, L. W. 1986. *Feuerstein's Cognitive Education Theory and American Indian Education.* ERIC Document Reproduction Services # ED276545 (Paper presented at the Mediated Learning Experience International Workshop).

FEUERSTEIN, R., Y. Rand, M. B. Hoffman and R. Miller. 1980. *Instrumental Enrichment, An Intervention Program for Cognitive Modifiability.* Baltimore, MD: University Park Press.

GREENBAUM, A. J., D. A. Chambers and J. Crawford. 1988. "Instrumental Enrichment Program: A Pilot Project," in *Eighth Yearbook of the College Reading Improvement Special Interest Group.* T. J. Betenbough and S. Biggs, eds. ERIC Document Reproduction Services # ED 303776, pp. 92–103.

HILLIARD, A. G. 1982. *The Learning Potential Assessment Device and Instrumental Enrichment as a Paradigm Shift.* Paper presented at the Annual Meeting of the American Educational Research Association. Eric Document Reproduction Services # ED223674.

LINK, F. R. 1985. "Instrumental Enrichment: A Strategy for Cognitive and Academic Improvement," in *Essays on the Intellect.* F. Link, ed. Alexandria, VA: Association for Supervision and Curriculum Development, pp. 89–106.

LINK, F. R. July 1990. Personal communication.

NICKERSON, R. S., D. N. Perkins and E. E. Smith, eds. 1985. *The Teaching of Thinking.* Hillsdale, NJ: Lawrence Erlbaum.

SAVELL, J. 1986. "Empirical Status of Feuerstein's Instrumental Enrichment Technique as a Method of Teaching Thinking Skills," *Review of Educational Research*, 56(4):381–409.

SAVELL, J. M. 1986. *Empirical Status of Feuerstein's Instrumental Enrichment as a Method of Teaching Thinking Skills*. Alexandria, VA: Army Research Institute for the Behavioral and Social Sciences.

SILVERMAN, H. 1988. "Feuerstein's Instrumental Enrichment Elicitation of Cognitive Interaction in the Classroom," *Canadian Journal of Special Education*, 4(2):133–150.

STERNBERG, R. 1985. "Approaches to Intelligence," in *Thinking and Learning Skills: Research and Open Questions, Volume 2*. S. F. Chipman, J. W. Segal and R. Glasser, eds. Hillsdale, NJ: Lawrence Erlbaum, pp. 232–243.

STERNBERG, R. J. and J. B. Baron, eds. 1987. *Teaching Thinking Skills, Theory and Practice*. New York: W. H. Freeman.

CoRT

The author of the CoRT program is Edward de Bono. Lateral thinking is the term which is most commonly associated with the CoRT (Cognitive Research Trust) thinking skills program. Lateral thinking is generally taken to mean creative thinking, that is, generating of possibilities—ideas which may be unconventional and not necessarily logical. Lateral thinking is a different process from vertical thinking, which is generally taken to mean systematic, logical thinking. The two types of thinking go hand in hand if the definitions are summarized as "Lateral thinking generates the ideas and vertical thinking develops them" (de Bono, cited in Nickerson, p. 215). Lateral thinking, in this sense, involves new ways of looking at a problem; vertical thinking involves delving deeper into an already established way of looking at the problem.

Operacy is another term which de Bono uses in a specific way. He identifies operacy as "the skill of doing things, of making things happen" (in Costa, 1985, p. 202). In this regard, information is no substitute for thinking, and thinking is no substitute for information. If there must be a choice, schools should spend less time in teaching information, i.e., facts, and spend more time in teaching thinking skills. Perception then becomes the crucial area in thinking. Perception, in de Bono's use, means "the way our minds make sense of the world around us" (1985, p. 204).

The other essential element (in addition to operacy) in de Bono's course is awareness. Awareness is considered a matter of insight as to what goes on in thinking.

De Bono's 1979 *Practical Thinking* adds further explanations to his background thinking about processes and skills which, at the time, were insufficient in his opinion. In the introduction to the book, he states that "...the most optimistic thing about the human race is its relative stupidity. There would be little hope if the human race was as bright as it thinks it is and still got itself into so much trouble" (p. 9). He further makes the generalization that at that time in England, more professors were concerned with antiquated languages than with thinking as a skill. De Bono set out to change that situation.

Program Criteria

A good thinking skills program, according to de Bono (1985, p. 206) should include several facets:

(1) The program should not require complicated teacher training.
(2) The program should be able to withstand damage in transfer from trainer to trainer and from trainer to teachers to students.
(3) The program should contain safeguards against the omission of skills; repetition of skills at different levels should be included.
(4) The program should be enjoyable for both students and teachers.
(5) The program should focus on thinking skills that also help a student to function better in life outside of school.

CoRT Tools

Tools are the thinking skills that students practice in CoRT lessons. Acronyms are used as mnemonic (memory-triggering) devices. Once students master the tools, they are encouraged to use them in all subjects. The tools of CoRT summarized (de Bono, 1982, pp. 18–151) include:

PMI: P stands for Plus (the good points), M stands for Minus (the bad points), I stands for the Interesting points about a problem. The explanation following the PMI description includes techniques for generating alternatives, being perceptive, identifying patterns, and using humor.

CAF means Consider All Factors and is designed to counter the supposed natural tendency of humans to be egocentric.

C&S stands for Consequence and Sequel and is designed to assist the student in thinking of long-term possibilities, as opposed to the usual impulsive response.

EBS stands for Examine Both Sides.

ADI stands for Agreement, Disagreement and Irrelevance.

OPV stands for Other People's Views.

HV stands for High Values, from the student's point of view of values.

LV stands for Low Values, again from the student's point of view.

AGO stands for Aims, Goals and Objectives, used in regard to decision-making.

TEC stands for Target and Task; E stands for Expand and Explore; C stands for Contract and Conclude. This took is meant to encourage more deliberate thinking.

PISCO stands for Purpose Input Solutions Choice Operations.

The CoRT tools have deliberately strange-sounding names in order to make them separate from content as attention-directors (de Bono, 1982, p. 15). The tools are practiced on a wide range of situations described on individual student work cards. Each situation is only considered for a short burst of time (2 to 4 minutes). Then the thinker applies the tool to another matter. This process is purported to be most effective in keeping attention on the tool rather than on the content. Once the tool is mastered, the skill can theoretically be applied to mastery of content in various subjects. If students understand the landscape of thinking, it supposedly becomes easier to find their way around the landscape. The tools, then, are the transportation for getting around the landscape.

Rationale

The Foreward to *Teaching Thinking* (de Bono, 1976) indicates that the author wishes the book "to be a gentle book that . . . upsets no one and gives help and encouragement to those who have always felt that thinking could be taught directly as a skill." But de Bono continues with an unusual statement in concluding that the book "will be seen as arrogant and dogmatic." This "dogmatic" approach apparently refers to his supposed ignoring of others' work in teaching thinking skills and the attacking of "sacred cows." His approach is justified in the statement "I cannot avoid it without diluting the purpose of the book" (p. 7). In summarizing, a defense is made in that his work is not to be interpreted as attacking logic, but that he views logic only as the processing stage of thinking. De Bono does make similar statements, as do other authors of thinking skills programs in treating thinking as "a skill that can be improved by attention" (1976, p. 10).

De Bono compares the teaching of thinking to walking a tightrope; it is easy if you do not fall off (1976, p. 16). That is, thinking is intangible and often awkward.

De Bono, as do authors of other thinking skills programs, stresses the necessity of developing active rather than passive students. His approach to teaching thinking stresses what educators call a divergent (creative) view of thinking as opposed to convergent (guided toward a preconceived goal) thinking. He developed the CoRT program to enhance the quality and quantity of thinking in schools. He calls the traditional mode of education a self-fulfilling prophecy in producing brilliant university graduates when only the students who perform the most brilliantly on specifically designed exams are admitted to universities in the first place. This is termed the "archway effect" by de Bono (1976, p. 13). In other words, if a stream of brilliant people go under an archway, then from that archway will emerge a stream of brilliant people. The archway has done no more than straddle their passage, to paraphrase his analogy. The implication is that in this regard, education has not really stretched the minds of most people, but has only reinforced the intellectual skills that have been used in typical elementary and secondary schools.

De Bono cautions that thinking should not be a replacement for gut feeling, religious belief, political identity or commitment. The teaching of thinking should therefore be neutral. In this context, thinking skills are kept as content-free as possible. In teaching thinking as a separate subject, de Bono's rationale is similar to Feuerstein's, even though the programs are structured differently. The learning of thinking skills is described by de Bono as similar to the use of a microscope in that both are devices to enlarge our vision. De Bono makes other conclusions similar to those of Feuerstein about the measurement of IQ, points out that a person with a high IQ is not necessarily *always* a good thinker, and challenges the belief that a person with a low IQ *cannot* be a good thinker (1976, p. 45). For example, there are many people who are so well informed within their own specialty that they are classed as brilliant. Outside that specialty, according to de Bono (1976, p. 33), their ability is reduced because they have less information to call upon. In other words, the mastery of information, i.e. facts, does not guarantee brilliance in the sense that is needed for today's world.

In defining thinking, de Bono states: "There is no one satisfactory definition of thinking . . . most definitions are satisfactory at one level or other." He includes as important such concepts as mental activity, logic, and reason, but stressed that they are *not sufficient* in and of themselves. The working definition that he uses in his 1976 rationale is "Thinking is the deliberate exploration of experience for a purpose" (p. 32). That purpose includes, but is not limited to, understanding, decision making, planning, problem solving, judgment and action. The purpose of thinking is to prepare something for us to feel about; the purpose of thought is to prepare us for action (p. 41). Thus emotion is an essential element in de Bono's view of human thinking.[14]

By 1982, a somewhat different definition of thinking is used: "Thinking is the operating skill with which intelligence acts upon experience (for a purpose)" (de Bono, 1982, p. 10). The bracket is added as a qualifier because not all thinking has a heavy sense of purpose, according to de Bono. This (1982) definition focuses on (1) operating skills, (2) intelligence, and (3) experience.

In identifying examples of good thinking in children, de Bono's rationale is similar to Lipman's although the programs developed to teaching thinking skills are very different. De Bono (1976, p. 37) relates an example of a nine-year-old's thinking:

"Can God do anything?"
"Yes, of course."
"Can he make a stone?"
"Yes, and anything else."
"Can he make a heavy stone?"
"As heavy as he likes."
"Can he make a stone so heavy that God can't lift it?"

The reasoning of the nine-year-old is quite complex, yet is not based on facts/information which would typically be learned in school. The thinking demonstrated is divergent, rather than convergent.

Language, notation and mathematics are deemed artificial aids to thinking by de Bono (1969, p. 19). If follows, then, that a more functional aid to thinking is needed. In developing CoRT tools, that need for a functional aid is supposedly fulfilled.

A BRIEF HISTORY OF THE PROGRAM

The name of the CoRT thinking skills program comes from the initials of the Cognitive Research Trust which was established in Cambridge, England, in 1973. Edward de Bono is the founder and remains the director of that organization.

The CoRT program (original and variations) has been used in a wide variety of settings in addition to schools. One of the youngest groups identified by de Bono (1976, p. 146) involved five-year-olds at a Unitarian Church in Britain; one of the adult groups involved IBM executives in France. Another group involved executives at Ford Motor Company in England. The IBM executives were using the program to learn English, as well as the thinking processes. Ability ranges of students identified by de Bono (1982, p. 13) include IQs from 75 to 150. The most frequent use of CoRT is in primary level school students of grades four through eight. De Bono identifies the preferred (target) ages 10–13.

Several thousand schools and approximately 6 million students in Canada, England, Ireland, Australia, New Zealand, Malta, Israel, Central and South America, Malaysia, Germany, Austria, France, and the U.S. are using CoRT Thinking Lessons (advertising brochure, 1984). The same basic lessons (with various adaptations) are used by ten-year-olds in the middle of the Venezuelan jungle as are used by gifted students in Canada and by executives in business organizations. Additional plans involve adapting CoRT for use in Cuba, China and Bulgaria (de Bono in Costa, 1985, p. 205).

DESCRIPTION OF MATERIALS

There are six sections to CoRT, each of which consists of ten lessons. One section is considered one term's work, one period of approximately 35 minutes per week (on the average). The entire course as designed covers three years.

CoRT Section I Breadth, emphasizes thinking about a situation in ways that ordinarily would not be considered.

CoRT Section II Organization, is designed to help the student direct attention systematically to a situation, without loss of focus.

CoRT Section III Interaction, deals with argument and adequate evidence.

CoRT Section IV Creativity, includes a number of strategies for generating ideas, evaluating and editing of ideas.

CoRT Section V Information and Feelings, deals with a variety of matters, some involving affective elements, and some involving review of earlier themes.

CoRT Section VI Action, involves a general framework for solving problems.

There is a teacher's handbook for each of the six sections and lesson notes for each pupil.

Teacher's Handbooks include:

Perspective, background and theory relating to teaching thinking skills in general and to CoRT in particular.

Teaching method, teaching points, difficulties and problems.

Additional practice items for testing purposes and as lesson supplements.

Teaching procedure and format for each section.

Detailed teaching notes for each lesson in the section.

Possible answers to problems are included; however, they are not to be construed by the teacher as the only answers possible. It is also suggested that teachers supplement examples and illustrations with local examples as appropriate.

Many of the CoRT operations overlap in a philosophical sense, although they are designed as practical tools rather than philosophical classifications (de Bono, 1976, p. 120).

RESEARCH REGARDING EFFECTIVENESS

Much of the research regarding the effectiveness of CoRT is reported in anecdotal form. That is, many examples are given of conversations with teachers and students in which verbal praise of the program's effects is presented, but little is available regarding statistical analysis of improved performance on specific tests of reasoning or correlated with increased standardized achievement tests.[15]

Several experiments involving generation of ideas are reported by de Bono (1976, pp. 217–229). In those studies, CoRT trained students produced considerably more ideas; some students also demonstrated a more balanced and less egocentric view of problems than did non-trained students. That is, CoRT trained students tended to give more attention to all sides of an issue, considering general as well as personal consequences.

Another study (Nickerson, p. 217) involving grade 10 science students in an all-boys school in Australia also indicated that CoRT trained students were more proficient in generating ideas and considering all sides of an issue after a term of training in the program. (There was no control group in this study.) Students who scored better on science exams after a term of CoRT training were students who also scored better on a measure of increased proficiency in CoRT. That is, the students who were more proficient in CoRT after a term of training were also better performers on their final term exam in science. That does not necessarily mean that better CoRT performance caused better science exam scores, but that some other factors such as general motivation to succeed in school may have been a factor for those students in improving scores in both CoRT and science classes.

The issue of transfer of CoRT skills into other subjects, according to de Bono (1976, pp. 116–117), depends largely upon whether the teacher reminds students to do so. In any regard, there has not been the development of a statistically validated test designed to assess that the students who receive CoRT training are learning thinking skills in the same ways that Philosophy for Children and Instrumental Enrichment have been tested. Despite the lack of statistically designed studies, the program has been adopted as part of the regular curriculum for public schools grades four, five, and six in Venezuela and is widely used in the U.S. and Canada.

Achievement Expectations

De Bono (in Costa, 1985, p. 208) identifies four levels of achievement expected of students in acquiring thinking skills from the CoRT program. Those skills (summarized) involve:

Level 1: A general awareness of thinking as a skill and a willingness to explore ideas.

Level 2: A more structured approach to thinking, including examining consequences and taking other people's views into account.

Level 3: Focused and deliberate use of some of the CoRT tools in organizing thinking.

Level 4: Fluent and appropriate use of many of the CoRT tools, i.e., the metacognitive level of thinking.

Average attainment of students reportedly fails somewhere between levels 1 and 2. Only in exceptional groups with very structured training does de Bono indicate that level 4 attainment is the average.

Another aspect of achievement is identified as the positive self-image that a student attains as "a thinker." This positive image is purported to be a major transfer effect to other subjects.

One report of The Valley Stream, New York, Junior High School indicates that concentrated attempts are being made to transfer the tools of CoRT to traditional classes (Melchior, Kaufold, and Edwards, 1988, p. 32). English teachers are sometimes using the tools for literary analysis; social studies teachers are asking students to use the tools to analyze the objectives of a government. In science, CoRT tools can be used to analyze issues in ecology and conservation. In addition, efforts have been made to extend the use of CoRT into departmental meetings with teachers and administrators. But again, data regarding specific areas of improved thinking have yet to be reported. The school initiated CoRT in 1982. A five-year research study was begun in 1986, but no details of the study design are yet available.

IMPLEMENTATION PROCEDURES

Teacher Training

"There can be no doubt that the successful teaching of thinking as a skill depends very largely on the teacher" (de Bono, 1976, p. 231). The teacher must believe in the program and must be determined to make it work. De Bono describes CoRT as usable by teachers who represent a wide range of abilities, not just the highly gifted.

Formal training, though optional, can be obtained in the form of workshops for teachers.[16]

Teachers are not directed to completely avoid grading the lessons; test items are provided so that students and teachers can assess their progress in comparison to the test items. Teachers are encouraged to verbalize praise for interesting or original ideas raised by students. Teachers are also free to criticize ideas, particularly if a student seems not to be taking the lesson seriously in giving obviously trivial or silly responses.

Time Required of Students

One period of thirty to fifty minutes per week is to be spent on CoRT lessons. A typical lesson has five stages (Chance, 1986, p. 17):

(1) In the introduction the teacher distributes the booklet called "Notes" that describes the tool to be learned and provides practice items for the tool.

(2) In the practice stage, students use the tool under study in small groups. One to five minutes are spent on discussion within the groups, then the teacher calls on individuals for ideas. There is not to be a general discussion, and debates are to be avoided. The

teacher may write comments from students on the board. Before the students have exhausted the possibilities of the practice item, the teacher turns their attention to the second item. Usually only two or three practice items from a choice of five per card are selected by the teacher for students to do.

(3) In the process stage, the entire class discusses the tool, i.e., process being studied. The teacher is directed to keep the pace brisk, and to see that the discussion does not get "bogged down" in philosophical "meanderings."

(4) In the principles stage, students again work in groups, considering the five principles listed in the booklet. The teacher directs students to perform a task concerning the principles. This stage is to last no more than five minutes.

(5) In the final stage, the project, students choose one of additional practice items from the booklet to consider. A maximum of fifteen minutes is spent in the stage. If time is short, the project may be assigned as homework or it may be incorporated into a different subject during the course of the school day.

Each lesson is devoted exclusively to one tool. Teachers are discouraged from reviewing tools covered earlier. De Bono believes that tools are best learned in isolation from one another.

Time allotted to the program most often comes from English classes, according to de Bono (1976, p. 155), but it is also used as part of religious instruction and moral education in other schools. Other appropriate areas for incorporating the lessons include social studies, humanities, and ESL (English as a Second Language) classes.

Costs

Sections I–V
Teacher's Handbooks, approximately $17.00
Workcards for Students, about $25.50 for packs of 100 cards.

Section VI
Teacher's Handbook, approximately $26.00

Students' Texts, about $11.50 each.

A complete set is approximately $250.00. An inspection package is available for approximately $18.00. It includes one copy of the CoRT I Teacher's Handbook and one copy of the 10 Workcards for CoRT I.[17]

ENDNOTES

13. In the closing remarks in the Foreward of *Teaching Thinking*, the reader is instructed to "take from the book whatever constructive ideas he may find rather than regarding it as a source of philosophical points with which he can enjoy disagreeing." This reflects a tone which often runs through de Bono's works. CoRT has been adapted by Sydney Tyler, in cooperation with Dr. de Bono, for use in U.S. Department of Defense Schools in pre-school and elementary classrooms. This adaptation is used in several districts in the U.S. and Canada. Called *Just Think* and *Stretch Think*, information regarding this series is available through: Thomas Geale Publications, Inc., 1142 Manhattan Avenue, Drawer C. P. 223, Manhattan Beach, CA 90266, (213) 379–4405.

14. de Bono has written extensively about his theories of thinking. If one book were chosen to read as background to his program, *Teaching Thinking* is probably the most thorough yet fairly readable.

15. I have found that in personal interviews, teachers who use CoRT are quite enthusiastic despite the lack of statistical analysis of effectiveness of thinking skills as taught through CoRT.

16. In one instance, teachers in Moose Jaw, Saskatchewan, utilized a satellite hookup and video interaction for workshop training.

17. For a descriptive brochure and current prices of materials, write to Dormac, Inc., P.O. Box 270459, San Diego, CA 92128–0983, (800) 547–8032 or Dominie Press Limited, 1361 Agincourt, Ontario MIS 3J1, Canada.

REFERENCES

BRODINSKY, B. 1985. "Tackling Problems through Lateral Thinking. An Interview with Edward de Bono," *School Administrator*. 42(3):10–13. (March).

CHANCE, P. 1986. *Thinking in the Classroom: A Survey of Programs*. New York: Teachers College Press.

COSTA, A., ed. 1985. *Developing Minds: A Resource Book for Teaching Thinking*. Association for Supervision and Curriculum Development.

DE BONO, E. 1969. *The Mechanism of Mind*. Middlesex, England: Penguin Books.

DE BONO, E. 1976. *Teaching Thinking*. London: Temple Smith.

DE BONO, E. 1979. *Practical Thinking*. Middlesex, England: Penguin Books.

DE BONO, E. 1982. *de Bono's Thinking Course*. Published to accompany the BBC TV series with same name. Bath, England: Pitman Press.

GRICE, G. L. 1987. *Instructional Strategies for the Development of Thinking Skills*. ERIC Document Resource # ED 287 185. (Paper presented at the Annual Meeting of the Speech Communication Association, Boston)

MELCHIOR, T. M., R. E. Kaufold and E. Edwards. 1988. "Using CoRT Thinking in Schools," *Educational Leadership*, 45(7):32–33.

NICKERSON, R. S., D. N. Perkins and E. E. Smith, eds. 1985. *The Teaching of Thinking*. Hillsdale, NJ: Lawrence Erlbaum.

TYLER, S. B. 1988. *Just Think*. Manhattan Beach, CA: Thomas Geale.

Structure of Intellect

OVERVIEW

The Structure of Intellect (SOI) program is based on a theory of intelligence developed by J. P. Guilford and colleagues (Nickerson, Perkins, and Smith, 1985, p. 162). The categorization of SOI as a thinking skills program is controversial. The reason for the controversy appears to be in program usage rather than in the choice of materials. SOI includes components for teaching creative and critical thinking, but apparently is more often used for diagnostic purposes and individualized instruction, rather than as curriculum for general classroom use. The authors of the program, Mary Meeker and Robert Meeker, differentiate between basic and higher-level critical thinking abilities as similar to differentiating between basic reading and advanced reading skills (M. Meeker, 1985, Chapter 30). The term "creativity" is used in a way which is similar to other authors of thinking skills programs.

The teaching methodology for younger students in the SOI program comes from the S–R (Stimulus–Response, or Behavioristic) psychological theory of learning (Meeker, 1976, p. b), that is, the program format has lessons with small steps, is very structured, and is thus controlled by the teacher.

The SOI program has been in systematic use since 1962 (Meeker, 1987, p. 4) and now contains materials suitable for use with students from kindergarten through adult.

The program purportedly covers all ranges of thinking skills, so teachers who wish to may utilize it for developing students' thinking abilities in the arts, math and language arts.

Guilford and colleagues spent approximately fifteen years (1944–1959) in developing the theory of intelligence that SOI utilizes. The theory is unique in its detail. Fifteen dimensions of intelligence are identified in the theory, each with several categories (M. Meeker, 1987,

p. 3). Intelligence is described in terms of the intersections of (a) five mental operations, (b) four contents, and (c) six products (Meeker, 1987, p. 4). The mental operations are cognition, memory, evaluation, convergent production and divergent production. The contents are figural, symbolic, semantic and behavioral. The products are units, classes, relations, systems, transformations and implications.

The SOI model as developed by Meeker purports to capture the full range of human abilities as represented in Guilford's theory of intelligence. Materials have been developed for students to develop each factor of intelligence in order to improve performance.[18]

Twenty-six of the intellectual abilities identified by SOI testing are claimed to be highly predictive of success in school. These abilities are measured on the Structure of Intellect-Learning Abilities Test (SOI-LA). Some of the abilities are involved in language arts, others are involved in arithmetic and math and yet another group of abilities involve creativity.

Use of the SOI materials is fairly straightforward. The first step is to obtain and administer a battery of SOI diagnostic tests. The test most often used is the SOI-LA. The second step is for the student(s) to complete individualized instruction in SOI materials and supplements. The third step is a post-test (same as the pre-test) to measure students' gains. The premise is that students will have much higher post-test scores after SOI training. The higher test score then indicates greater potential for classroom achievement.

The program is described as more "teacher-proof" than other thinking skills programs because of its test-like nature, but that there is "probably less transfer" to other subjects because of the design which "teaches to the test" (Sternberg and Bhana, October, 1986, pp. 64–66). The program does not have bridging material built into it as do other thinking skills programs, according to Sternberg and Bhana. Nor does the program depend entirely upon class discussion as do Philosophy for Children (extensively), Instrumental Enrichment (somewhat extensively) and CoRT (less extensively). Meeker (1990) however, contends that these conclusions are false because "the test does not look like any of the materials."

Critical Thinking Abilities as Identified in SOI Curriculum

Summarized from Meeker, 1987, (pp. 188–191):

Reading Category:

Analytic Reasoning (criticism and text analysis)

Inferential Reasoning
Deductive Reasoning (verbal logic)
Inductive Reasoning (hypothesis generation)
Decision Making

Arithmetic and Mathematics:

Analytical Reasoning (symbolic translation)
Inferential Reasoning (problem solving, debugging)
Deductive Reasoning (symbolic logic, notational language)
Decision Making (program design)

Rationale

Meeker is in accord with other authors of thinking skills programs in indicating that "students need to learn far more than the basic skills . . . an education should prepare a (person) for work that doesn't yet exist and whose nature cannot even be imagined" (M. Meeker, 1976, p. a). This is accomplished, according to Meeker, by "giving them the kind of intellectual discipline that will enable them to apply man's accumulated wisdom to new problems . . ." (1976, p. a).

The program is often taught separately from other school subjects; often on a one-to-one basis. An underlying assumption is that all students have intelligence. The SOI program answers "What kind?" instead of "How much?" (Meeker, 1985, p. 187). The program is designed to lay the basic foundation for sequencing learning abilities. Once basic abilities are mastered, theoretically, higher-level reasoning or critical thinking abilities are more easily assimilated. The extent of critical thinking by students is thus affected by use of knowledge of subject matter.

Meeker (1985, p. 192) believes that it is necessary to separate verbal and quantitative preparation for critical thinking.

The rationale can be summarized as having the goal of equipping students with the necessary intellectual skills to learn subject matter and critical thinking.

A BRIEF HISTORY OF THE PROGRAM

In Meeker's book (1969), the foundation for the SOI program is explained in terms of educational applications.

The SOI Institute was located for many years in El Segundo, California, but has now relocated in Vida, Oregon (see author notes for address).

The ideas basic to SOI theory were developed and revised in the late 1950s (Meeker, 1969, p. 8). The first experimental draft to validate SOI with students was published in Los Angeles in 1963 (Meeker, p. 112). The pilot study involved gifted children grades 2–6. Field testing and revisions periodically took place until the present (1969) model was outlined. Meeker (p. 155) includes descriptions of a series of sample, individualized SOI profiles and interpretations selected from over a thousand children profiled in the U.S. and Canada. Student populations for the profiles include: gifted, normal range IQ, mentally retarded, educationally handicapped, blind-from-birth, behaviorally handicapped males, and highly anxious students.

Some of the questions that a teacher faces, as a result of a student profile are (1) Do I teach to a strength? and (2) Do I teach to a deficit? Teachers historically teach to student deficits. It may be this practice which causes teachers to inadvertently skip some of the creative aspects of using SOI. If students' strengths are not equally treated, then it is very possible that the highest achievement potentials are not being reached. This summarizes what appears to be the greatest danger in such a prescriptive program as SOI.

Meeker claims (p. 183) that prior to Guilford, education lacked a formal theory of intelligence around which curriculum could be developed. SOI, as a program built around a theory of intelligence, is called "cognitive therapy" by Meeker (p. 184). Therapy is a term which is not generally associated with traditional classroom teaching. That association may or may not be valid; more use of the program in traditional classrooms is needed before detailed historical comparisons to other thinking skills programs can be made.

DESCRIPTION OF MATERIALS

Each SOI lesson is called a prescription. Within the directives for the lessons are terms for the use of the teacher, counselor or psychologist, who may be using the program for very precise individualized instruction. There is also a learning objective stated on each page, which describes intellectual abilities to be achieved in that lesson. Teachers may choose to teach these objectives to students as terminology. This would be to help them become aware of the terms for abilities which are used in measuring intelligence. (If so taught, however, this is teaching factual knowledge as opposed to reasoning skill.) Each lesson also provides a space to record student progress. Teachers may (1) record the predicted level of development that is expected from the student, and (2) may indicate the amount of student change (positive or negative) in that area. Evaluation in this sense is a judgment which is more or less precise, depending upon the standard set for each objective by the teacher.

The Structure of Intellect-Learning Abilities (SOI-LA) Tests

Cognition (Comprehension)

There are eighteen specific kinds of cognition in Guilford's theory; nine are tested on the SOI-LA Test (Meeker, 1987, p. 5). Meeker does not include the six behavioral products because they have not factored successfully (Meeker, 1990).

The Assessment

(a) Comprehensive Form for approximately grade 2 to adult—Contains twenty-six subtests for assessing discrete abilities (intellectual functions). Provides fourteen general ability scores ranging from the disabling to gifted level. Time: 2½ hours.

(b) Gifted Screening Form. Time: 1 hour. Consists of eleven of the twenty-six abilities most predictive of grades and achievement.

(c) Reading/Language Arts Form—Appropriate for, approximately, grades 7 and up. Designed for students who are experiencing difficulty in reading and language arts activities. Assesses intellectual functioning in the abilities required and profiles these abilities for identification of strengths and weaknesses. Time: 1 hour.

(d) Arithmetic/Math Skills for, approximately, grades 7 and up—Considers each of the intellectual functions required to master both arithmetic and math. Provides a profile of the student's strengths and weaknesses. Time: 1 hour.

(e) Process and Diagnostic Screening Test Form P for grades K–3—Consists of eleven subtests. Provides a profile of strengths and weaknesses in basic reading skills and cognitive style (measures figural, symbolic and semantic abilities). Time: 1½–2 hours.

(f) Reading Readiness Form: R.R. for grades K–2 – Measures skills basic for reading and thinking. Designed for use with young children and new readers. Time: 1 hour.

The resulting profile provides a diagnostic analysis, for which individual training programs can be developed. Specific learning materials are identified. Purpose of training:

(a) as preparation for acquiring curriculum content
(b) as remedial and development for the student with learning difficulties
(c) as enrichment for the student who wishes to explore new types of thinking and reasoning skills.

Note: It is possible for parents to obtain a specific program for at-home use. The sourcebooks offer lesson plans and activities over a wide range of subjects. Meeker (1987, p. 5) indicates that it does, however, require effort to acquire all the diverse materials needed for the lessons. The training modules are described as game-like books that allow children and adults to work independently at their own pace.

Cognition Comprehension Tasks that teachers or parents can use include:

(1) Identifying objects by name
(2) Classifying pictures, words and numbers
(3) Finding relationships between items
(4) Decoding of complex relationships of items, patterns or systems
(5) Transferring figures into other shapes, gradually increasing difficulty level (Montessori materials are suggested as useable, as well as martial arts and sports which help to integrate both sides of the body.)
(6) Following instructions of increasing complexity
(7) Teaching and asking for several meanings to a word or expression
(8) Predicting consequences
(9) Learning new and unusual words (Meeker, 1969, 1980)

Memory

There are eighteen kinds of memory identified by Guilford; five are tested on the SOI-LA Test.

Tasks that teachers and parents can use:

(1) Recall of material learned by visual, tactile or auditory presentation

(2) Recall arrangement of objects shown then removed

(3) Recall, after one or two second presentations, a series of numerals or letters

(4) Drills in types of mathematics operations, a maximum of 10 minutes per sitting

(5) Recall of ideas from a paragraph which is read to them

(6) Making up problems for others to solve

(7) Sight memory of words by location on a page and meaning of words

(8) Recall of related pairs of words

(9) Recall of the order of events and prediction of next event

(10) Music and foreign language training (Meeker, 1969, 1980)

Evaluation (Judging, Planning, Decision Making, Analysis, Reasoning and Logic)

There are eighteen kinds of evaluation abilities in Guilford's theory, four are tested on the SOI-LA Test.
Evaluation tasks that teachers and parents can use include:

(1) Making judgments about sorting and classifying

(2) Identifying defects or absurdities in spatial, numerical or semantic problems

(3) Finding related numbers in a numerical series

(4) Practicing logic in testing conclusions

(5) Appraising situations in terms of experience

(6) Receiving practical judgments about ideas presented (*Innovative Science*, Lipman's *Philosophy for Children* program and Arthur Whimley's books are described as being excellent supplements for training in this area.) (Meeker, 1969, 1980, 1990)

Convergent Production (Problem Solving where Answers Are Known)

There are eighteen different kinds of problem solving in Guilford's theory, four are tested on the SOI-LA Test.
Convergent production tasks that parents and teachers can use include:

(1) Reproducing figures and mimicking exercises

(2) Sorting pictures, words or numerals into major categories (Golden Science Books or collecting coins, minerals, or stamps are suggested as useful)

(3) Solving deductive problems

(4) Filling in blanks in numeral series or sentences

(5) Solving simple equations orally

(6) Stating the order of symbolic systems

(7) Correctly naming concepts or ideas

(8) Showing relations between ideas

(9) Computer programming

(10) Solving jigsaw and crossword puzzles (Meeker, 1969, 1980)

Divergent Production (Creative Problem Solving)

There are 18 kinds of creative problem solving identified in Guilford's theory, three are tested on the SOI-LA Test.[20]

Divergent production tasks that teachers and parents can use include:

(1) Reclassifying objects, pictures, numbers and words in unusual ways

(2) Generating a variety of relations between numbers, letters or ideas

(3) Brainstorming ideas, creative writing by hand or on a computer

(4) Producing words from given synonyms or associated words

(5) Producing "clever" titles, describing uncommon ways of using common objects

(6) Brainstorming (without value judgement) about results; altering solutions

(7) Videotaping their own stories acted out by friends or classmates

(8) Participating in dramas, art, dance and other hands-on experiences (Meeker, 1969, 1980)

RESEARCH REGARDING EFFECTIVENESS

The tasks in the SOI workbooks, according to Meeker (1976, Introduction) have been used and tested with students having abilities including gifted, slow learning, mentally retarded, disadvantaged, educationally handicapped, average, neurologically impaired, bilingual and with various ethnic mixes. Meeker concludes that the evidence indicates that children's intelligence can be trained, and if trained specifically, can also result in improved self-concept and improved attitudes toward school in general.

A study of 147 gifted secondary science students (Subotnik, April, 1988, p. 42) supported the predictive value of SOI. In that study, SOI was used to assist students in choosing their research questions, a problem-solving assistance. Another study with twelfth grade Physics students in Florida indicated that SOI was similar to the Florida State-Wide Twelfth Grade Test in predicting physics achievement (Ignatz, 1982, p. 935). The predictive value may be of use to some schools, and of little or no interest to other schools, depending on the goal of the task.

A Laredo, Texas study (1981) indicated some gender differences, in comparing scores on SOI. Tenth grade Hispanic males and females showed significant differences in 5 of 11 scores in arithmetic computation. The conclusion was that a differentiated curriculum seems to be needed. In addition, some of the results indicated that seventh grade males and females scored significantly below most SOI norms in basic reading skills, advanced reading skills, and arithmetic computational skills.

Another study (Laine and Wong, 1982, p. 263) involved 23 eighth grade students identified as having potential learning problems. The conclusion to this study indicated that the SOI test was effective in assisting educators in identifying, diagnosing and aiding students toward greater school achievement.

A study (Pearce, 1983, p. 13) involving gifted fifth- and sixth-grade students was not positive toward SOI. The conclusion was that Raven's Matrices was a more significant predictor of intelligence than the SOI Screening Form for Gifted.[19]

SOI was used for promoting the abilities of seventy-five "potentially gifted culturally different" students in grades 3–5 in Palm Beach, Florida (Howells, 1983, p. 4). Thirty-nine students made 10% or higher gains over previous scores on standardized achievement and IQ tests after implementing SOI prescribed curriculum. Conclusions were that the use of SOI was positive in this situation. Teachers also indicated satisfaction with students who then moved on to the "regular" gifted program.

The creative aspect of SOI (the divergent thinking scale) was sup-

ported by a study of fifty-three primary grade, gifted students (Severeide and Sugawara, 1985, p. 2). A six-month follow-up study indicated that all gains were maintained. Gender differences were found
that showed that girls increased more on the verbal measures in both
the control group and the experimental group, a factor not attributed to
SOI training in divergent thinking.

A different report indicated that the results of evaluation data provided by the SOI institute were "inconclusive." The report was conducted by the Jackson County Education Service District in Medford,
Oregon (1982). The study, with data about individualized SOI training
in learning and divergent thinking, involved (1) underachievers in the
general school population, (2) minority gifted students, and (3) gender
differences (using SOI summarized research). Specifically, the conclusion was that "the relationship of SOI and reading, writing, and creativity are not well supported or even very well discussed . . ." (p. 28). A
generalized conclusion of the Medford, Oregon, district about using
SOI is that the program works best in individualized situations. There
are reportedly management problems in using the program in a general
mainstream classroom. However, the use of SOI in classrooms can be
accomplished (with some additional effort) in small groups such as in
reading groups in elementary classrooms and perhaps in social studies
classes in upper grades.

Sternberg and Bhana (1984, p. 65) are among those who have criticized the research as disproportionately involving gifted students.
Meeker (1990) disputes their conclusion.

IMPLEMENTATION PROCEDURES

Teacher Training

There are three levels of training available from the SOI Institute.
The minimum for teachers is basic training.

In implementing the program, additional materials other than those
provided by SOI are necessary. Some districts have reportedly
managed with a half-time teacher's aide for this purpose, while other
districts have had one full-time teacher assigned to the program (Schofield, 1982, p. 40).

A sample schedule of events for a school which plans to fully integrate the SOI program (Schofield, p. 37) involves 4½ years:

- Allow six months to one year to get ready to use SOI (arrange a depository for materials; conduct teacher training).[21]
- Allow two years to get the program off the ground.
- Allow two years of usage before producing measurable, stable effects.

In summary, since SOI is diagnostic and prescriptive, teachers require training in (1) diagnostic procedures and (2) specific methodology for the program. In addition, retraining involves at least a two-day seminar (Meeker, 1985, p. 192).

Time Required of Students

Approximately 30-minute lessons are required twice a week until abilities develop sufficiently to require post-assessments. One semester of individualized tutoring may be sufficient; two years in the SOI program is not uncommon.

Costs

Basic two-day workshops for certification as Basic SOI trainers are held in Los Angeles or Eugene, Oregon. The cost is approximately $375 and includes all materials necessary to initiate and maintain a program.

Intermediate workshops (available only to those who have completed the Basic Workshop and have experience using SOI) are $200.00.

Advanced Workshops (available only by invitation) to certify trainers for staff development, program development, private centers and services are $200.

Awareness materials include:

- statistics & worksheet packet of norms, stanines, gifted and special education cutoff scores at approximately $10
- SOI Newsletter for $9 per year
- SOI-LA test forms and subtest forms are approximately $2.00 to $3.15 each.
- Sourcebooks are approximately $12.00 each.
- Creative Learning Workbooks are approximately $13 each; response cards are approximately $8.

- Computer disks are available to districts for in-house control. Computer analyses range from $15 to $25.
- Interpretation Guides for the SOI are approximately $16.
- The Handbook for Reasoning is $18, with transparencies for $45.

ENDNOTES

18. For information about the program and training, write to SOI Systems, P.O. Box D, Vida, OR 97488, (503) 896-3936.

19. A personal conversation with one psychometrist (B.A. and M.Ed. in counseling) indicated a disagreement with this conclusion; she indicated that SOI screening devices are much easier and more objective for her purposes in individualized tutoring programs.

20. This "major" ability is rarely included as a part of school curriculum, according to Meeker (p. 7). This is the portion of the SOI program involving activities most similar to other thinking skills programs.

21. A counselor or psychologist versed in testing procedures would find it advisable to read Meeker's (1969) *Structure of Intellect, Its Interpretation and Uses* as minimal background information regarding the program and testing rationale.

REFERENCES

BACHELOR, P. A. and B. G. Bachelor. 1989. "An Investigation of the Higher-Order Symbolic Factors of Cognition and Convergent Production within the Structure of Intellect Model," *Educational and Psychological Measurement*, 49:537–548.

HOWELLS, R. F. 1983. *Pilot Project for Potentially Gifted Minority Students.* ERIC document # ED 234564. West Palm Beach, FL: Palm Beach County Board of Public Instruction. (Paper presented at the Council for Exceptional Children National Conference on the Exceptional Black Child.)

IGNATZ, M. 1982. "A Comparison of Structure of Intellect Factors with the Florida State-Wide Twelfth Grade Test in Predicting Physics Achievement," *Educational and Psychological Measurement*, 42(3):935–939.

LAINE, C. J., and B. Y. Wong. 1982. "Identifying Differences in Learning Needs between Successful and Unsuccessful Secondary Students by the Structure of Intellect Test: An Exploratory Investigation," *British Columbia Journal of Special Education*, 6(3):263–276.

MEEKER, M. N. 1969. *The Structure of Intellect, Its Interpretation and Uses.* Columbis, OH: Charles E. Merrill.

MEEKER, M. July 1990. Personal communication.

PEARCE, N. 1983. "A Comparison of the WISC-P, Raven's Standard Progressive

Matrices, and Meeker's SOI-Screening Form for Gifted," *Gifted Child Quarterly*, 27(1)13–19.

SCOFIELD, S. J. 1982. *A Discussion of the Structure of Intellect Test and Curriculum Model*. ERIC document # ED 227122. Medford, OR: Southern Oregon Research and Development Committee.

SEVEREIDE, R. C. and A. I. Sugawara. 1985. *The Effectiveness of Creative Experiences in Enhancing Creative Development*. ERIC document # ED 258375.

SUBOTNIK, R. F. April 1988. "Factors from the Structure of Intellect Model Associated with Gifted Adolescents' Problem Finding in Science: Research with Westinghouse Science Talent Search Winners," *Journal of Creative Behavior*, 22(1):42–54.

TUEL, F. S. 1989. "Sex Differences on the Structure of Intellect (SOI-LA) Screening Form," *Gifted Child Quarterly*, 33(2):73–75.

Newer Programs

Programs, books, booklets, posters, computer programs—materials that claim to teach thinking—are popping up like crocus in springtime. Some of them have been carefully tended and nourished; others are little more than wild things springing up along roadsides. The programs summarized in this chapter give evidence of careful "cultivation." However, they have been in existence a relatively short time and therefore do not have as much information regarding effectiveness as do the programs in Chapters 3 through 6. Such conclusions/judgments as are available about the use of these materials in teaching thinking skills have been summarized for presentation in this chapter.[22]

HOTS

Overview

The Higher-Order Thinking Skills (HOTS) program was originally developed by Stanley Pogrow to help U.S. Chapter 1 students (Pogrow, 1985, p. 239). As such, HOTS is a pullout-type program (separate from the regular classroom) which combines computer activities with effective teaching methods in efforts to go beyond teaching only rote skills. An assumption of the program is that students have innate intelligence that can be developed by challenging them intellectually. The computer is used in the HOTS program (1) for its theoretically motivational aspects to students, and (2) because it enables students to get feedback on their ideas at the same speed at which they think. Current projects involve using the program with mainstream classrooms. Pilot projects have expanded to include learning disabled students in grades 4–6, gifted students in grades K–2, and Chapter 1 students in grade 7.

Thinking activities are organized in a manner which, based on research, the brain seems to follow in long-term storage of information. That is, the focus is on allowing students to develop their own strategies for associations of ideas rather than making them dependent on teacher-directed strategies. This makes HOTS a processing model (separate skills approach) rather than an infused into content approach.

Regarding at-risk students, Pogrow (1988, p. 80) is convinced that whatever thinking skills approach is used, a separate general thinking approach is much more effective than the infusion approach.

Materials

Information regarding HOTS is available from the developer:

Stanley Pogrow
College of Education
University of Arizona
Tucson, AZ 85721
(602) 621-1305

Implementation

The program requires a computer lab (Apple IIe, IIc or IIgs) and a "very good" teacher who is trained in shifting from teaching approaches such as lecturing and linear sequencing to Socratic coaching techniques (HOTS Information Pamphlet, 1989). Teacher training in the HOTS program involves approximately one week. Teachers practice-teach lessons from the curriculum to their peers. Coaching of techniques is an integral part of the training.

HOTS is usually implemented in grades 4-7. High quality teaching and structured curricular strategies are identified as essential (Pogrow, 1985, p. 238). An atmosphere of "assertive thinking" should pervade the HOTS classroom. The teacher's role becomes one of a guide for students, assisting them in (1) analyzing computer feedback and (2) making decisions about their ideas and strategies. An essential element of instruction in HOTS for at-risk students is that teachers facilitate understanding through extensive verbal conversations with students (Pogrow, 1988, p. 80). In that regard, teachers must learn a new set of strategies completely different from rote memory drill and practice, which are techniques common in remedial classes.

The HOTS curriculum provides a day-to-day script for teachers to use. Methods are identified for linking concepts and techniques (transfer, i.e., bridging) learned in computer usage to the regular classroom.

The recommended amount of student time in the program is thirty-five minutes per session, four days per week for two years.

Compared to Chapter 1 programs that use experienced teachers, the overall cost of the HOTS program is said to be less, even taking equipment costs into account.

Implementing HOTS in a typical school costs $750 for training, curriculum and support.

Research Regarding Effectiveness

HOTS began with a single pilot project; by 1990, 800 schools had adopted the program for Chapter 1 or LD students (Pogrow, 1990). Former U.S. Secretary of Education Terrell Bell awarded the program a grant as an outstanding national technology demonstration project.

HOTS has been evaluated positively in regard to Chapter 1 students using (1) standardized achievement tests, (2) Ross Test of Higher Order Thinking, (3) social confidence as measured by sociograms. 1988 research of projects involving rural, urban, and inner-city schools in the U.S. supports earlier studies (Pogrow, April, 1988, p. 79). The implication in the research is that enhanced thinking skills in HOTS students results more from the development of verbal understanding in language than from use of the computer. Use of computer programs alone, therefore, does not promote development of higher order thinking skills. Sophisticated conversations between students and teacher around what is happening on the computer is the key element (Pogrow, 1990).

HOTS has been endorsed by the U.S. Department of Education as having been used successfully in grades 4–7. The program is now disseminated by the National Diffusion Network.[23]

LOGO

Overview

LOGO is a computer language that is a vehicle for the student to use in interacting with the machine. As such, the computer is an extension of the user (Wiederhold, 1985, p. 255). The language of LOGO is purported to be natural for beginners in computer programming in exploring mathematical and logical concepts (Nickerson, Perkins, and Smith, 1985, p. 269). Lessons have been developed in syllogistic logic, number representations, functions and equations, and strategies for problem solving. The program has been used both for separate skills instruction and as part of mathematics classes. An assumption is that learning depends largely on relating new information to old. The LOGO "turtle" on the computer screen is related to the real world and is thus non-threatening to students. Subroutines in LOGO called PETAL and FLOWER are other examples of this premise.

LOGO users, principally Papert of the Massachusetts Institute of Technology (Nickerson et al., p. 273), also see the program as a means of fostering general thinking and learning skills. That is, the practices of programming and debugging programs are processes that provide the student with skills that s/he can transfer to the classroom and real world situations. The teacher should encourage students to make this transfer.[24]

Materials/Implementation

Various publications for teachers are available for using LOGO on different computers.[24]

Research Regarding Effectiveness

LOGO has been used both in mainstream classrooms and with mentally and physically handicapped students (Nickerson et al., p. 275). The research summarized primarily involved individual case studies. A generalization is that LOGO's "turtle" geometry can provide a model of concrete examples of abstractions such as angle and distance. Such examples seem to assist students' understanding of the concepts. However, the use of LOGO in developing students' general problem solving abilities or in being systematic is not well supported by research, despite teachers enthusiasm about such usage. One possible reason is that in-depth research on a long-term basis (more than one semester) has yet to be conducted (Robinson, 1984).

According to some proponents, LOGO need not be limited to use in elementary schools, but can be a valuable tool for college students; however, a 1987 study involving college students between the ages of eighteen and fifty-seven found that critical thinking skills were not affected by age, gender, or learning to program computers in LOGO (Sattler, 1987).

ODYSSEY: A CURRICULUM FOR THINKING

Odyssey is a program which was developed for use in Venezuela as part of that country's 1979 Project Intelligence. Odyssey is designed for use in mainstream (heterogeneously grouped) classrooms of upper elementary and middle schools. The primary authors of the program include David Perkins of Harvard University, and the consulting firm of Bolt, Beranek and Newman, Inc., with the Venezuelan Ministry of Education (Chance, 1986, p. 59).

Odyssey is a content-free approach which purports to teach a wide variety of intellectual tasks, including:

- deductive reasoning
- inductive reasoning
- the precise use of language
- inferential use of information in memory
- hypothesis generation
- hypothesis testing
- problem solving
- inventiveness and creativity
- decision making

A premise is that thinking skills are life skills, involving performance, communication, attitudes, and values.

Materials

There are teacher's manuals for approximately $20.00 each, teacher's resource books ranging from $55.00–$95.00, and student books ranging from $4.25–$5.25 each. Titles include:

- *Foundations of Reasoning*
- *Understanding Language*
- *Problem Solving*
- *Decision Making*
- *Inventive Thinking*

Included with *Decision Making* and *Inventive Thinking* Teachers' Manuals are Blackline Masters.

Lessons are to be approximately 45 minutes each, three to five times per week. The program as designed takes two years to complete.

Ordering information is available from the publisher:

Mastery Education Corporation
85 Main Street
Watertown, MA 02172
(617) 926-0329
(800) 225-3214

Implementation

Training is not required, but is available from the publisher of the program, Mastery Education Corporation. The teacher's manuals are fairly straightforward and explicit in directions for use.

Student participation includes both verbal (class discussion) and written exercises. Student worksheets are not to be formally graded.

Some of the lessons involve increasing students' abilities in using the knowledge they already have, while other lessons involve acquisition of new knowledge. The methodology is "deliberately eclectic" (Wright, 1985, p. 224). That is, a combination of dialectic and didactic teaching methods are used. Some lessons are based on a Socratic-like approach and other lessons are based on a Piagetian-style analysis of cognitive development. Still other lessons use a Bruner-like style of inquiry and discovery.

Research Regarding Effectiveness

No detailed studies regarding use in North America are available. However, the results of the Venezuelan study are positive (Chance, p. 70) and show increased student achievement on tests of thinking and on standardized tests. Odyssey is possibly a prime program for use with U.S. Chapter 1 students who have characteristics similar to many of the Venezuelan barrio schools where the socioeconomic status is low and parents have minimal expectations from schools (Adams, 1986). Similar conditions exist in low socioeconomic areas in Canada. This may be an excellent program for a school to use as a pilot project and it would perhaps be possible to obtain a grant for such a study.

PROBLEM SOLVING AND COMPREHENSION: A SHORT COURSE IN ANALYTICAL REASONING

Overview

Problem Solving and Comprehension, by Arthur Whimbey and Jack Lockhead, is designed for students from approximately junior high through the first college years, or as preparation for college. The program can be used alone or in combination with other material (Whimbey and Lockhead, 1980, p. 1). The goal of the program is more efficient reading and practice in the mental operations essential to analytical reasoning. The program purports to reinforce thinking patterns (1) that underlie success in solving math and science problems, (2) for mastering the content of academic courses and the requirements of technical occupations. The target audience includes students who are marginally qualified for the type of systematic, analytical thinking characteristic of students who are successful in college work.

Materials

The course begins with students taking the Whimbey Analytical Skills Inventory (WASI). This inventory provides insight into student thinking. Students analyze their test results and learn ways to avoid common errors. Demonstrations of correct problem examples are given, followed by individual practice.

There is one text/workbook. The text includes problems of verbal reasoning, analogical reasoning and speed reading, as well as the WASI.

The text costs approximately $14.00 and is available from

Lawrence Erlbaum, Inc.
365 Broadway
Hillsdale, NJ 07642
(201) 666-4110

Implementation

Between ten and forty hours are required to complete the book, depending on how many problems are worked. The format is usually a one-semester course, however, it is possible for a highly motivated student to go through the book independent of any instructor.

Students usually work in pairs and take turns in verbalizing their thought patterns in solving problems. The course can be designed as either remedial or enrichment. The instructor provides little more than an introduction to the format (including the WASI discussion), and a positive atmosphere. No formal training is required, although some workshops are provided as requested by schools.

Research Regarding Effectiveness

Our study involving Whimbey's program is called Project SOAR (Stress on Analytical Reasoning). Project SOAR involves a five-week pre-freshman program at Xavier University (a predominately black school) in New Orleans (Whimbey, 1985, p. 269). After using the pair problem-solving technique for several hours with word analogies, students shift over to math problems (including plane geometry and algebra) and reading comprehension. Exercises progress from simple to complex. Students reportedly have increased scores an average of two grade levels on the Nelson-Denny Reading Test, and an average gain of 110 points on the SAT after the course. In addition, SOAR students reportedly are twice as successful in passing freshman science and math courses as were similar students before the SOAR project.

Other studies are summarized by Whimbey (p. 271) as being positive about Problem Solving and Comprehension training with high school students, and adaptations are being developed for elementary grades. However a contradictory study involving eighty-five students at State University of New York at Albany reported no significant gains in reading comprehension over control groups receiving instruction in a speed reading course (Fennelly, 1988).

PRODUCTIVE THINKING

Overview

The Productive Thinking Program was developed over a twelve-year period by psychologists Martin Covington, Richard Crutchfield, Lillian Davies and Robert Olton, with the support of the Carnegie Corporation. More than ten thousand students in schools throughout the United States and Canada were involved in the process (Chance, 1986, p. 26).

The goal of the program is to teach students to use their minds "in an effective, intelligent, and creative way directed at the solution of the problem" (Segal and Chipman, 1985, Chapter 12).

In the words of Covington, "Intelligent behavior in school means acting to make a difficult assignment easier, redefining a problem . . . in light of new contingencies, and recognizing when one does not understand a concept. All these actions are governable by rules, and it is in this sense that intelligence can be modified and improved" (Covington, 1985, p. 410).

Students are taught sixteen thinking guides, i.e., strategies, for generalized problem-solving techniques. As such, it is a separate-skills approach, requiring both convergent and divergent thinking, and dependent upon motivated teachers to remind students to transfer the strategies into content areas.

Principles of problem solving include:

- idea generation
- persistence
- being systematic
- evaluation of ideas
- positive attitude

Materials

The lessons are presented in cartoon format in a series of fifteen booklets. A teacher's guide is available. In addition, a large wall chart is also provided as a reminder for students and teachers to use the "thinking guides" throughout the day.

For availability of materials, write to

Dr. Martin Covington
Department of Psychology
3210 Tolman Hall
University of California at Berkeley
Berkeley, CA 94720

Implementation

The program is designed to take approximately one semester to complete, a notably shorter length of time than that required of many other thinking skills programs.

The target grades for the program are mainstream fifth or sixth grades, but the materials are appropriate for either gifted or remedial students in other grades. The lessons can be used either individually or in groups. Class discussion is an element of the program.

Formal teacher training is not described as necessary; however, enthusiastic and systematic teaching is a requirement for implementing the teacher's guides.

Research Regarding Effectiveness

A great deal of research has been conducted in order to evaluate the effectiveness of the Productive Thinking program (Segal and Chipman, 1985, Chapter 12). The results are generally positive, with some exceptions. The program, like other thinking skills programs, is teacher-sensitive. Unless the teacher reminds students to use the thinking guides in content areas, the program is relatively ineffective for many students.

One of the more positive studies involved a 1983 Canadian study (Harris and Blank, 1983) using fifth-grade students. That study indicated that training in the program enhanced students' creative problem solving. In addition, teachers in the study indicated a preference for the Productive Thinking program over other infused approaches.

PROJECT IMPACT

Overview

IMPACT is an acronym for Improving Minimal Proficiencies by Activating Critical Thinking. The program author is S. Lee Winocur. The goal of the program is to increase students' performances in mathematics, reading, and language arts. The improvement is measured in terms of student achievement on district tests of basic competency, including tasks that require critical thinking (Winocur, 1985, p. 210). The program was originally designed as an alternative approach to remedial reading and math for junior and senior high schools, although adaptations have been made for K–college. The Howard County, Maryland, school, for one, has adapted the program for grades 2–5 (Shulik, April 1988, p. 41).

The methodology in IMPACT incorporates elements of effective (direct) instruction: (1) skills are clearly identified and sequenced hierarchically, (2) teacher behaviors are identified and practiced, (3) skills are presented in a lesson-plan format. The skills are not taught as a separate subject, but are infused into the regular course content. In addition, IMPACT purports to accommodate individual developmental stages and learning styles. Tasks are designed to move from the concrete to the abstract.

Thinking skills which Project IMPACT utilizes include:

- classifying and categorizing
- ordering
- identifying relevant information
- identifying irrelevant information
- inductive reasoning
- deductive reasoning
- rendering judgments

Materials

The IMPACT program Curriculum Materials Kits cost approximately $150.00 and contain handbooks for language arts and mathematics. Approximately sixty Language Arts/Social Studies and sixty Mathematics/Science teacher-developed sample lessons are included. One filmstrip is included in each kit. The program also has "Home Enrichment Learning Packets" that may be used to reinforce the aspects of skills identified as the most difficult for individual students to grasp.

Kit contents may be purchased separately: IMPACT Mathematics and Language Arts Handbooks cost $75.00 each. Filmstrip and audiotapes cost $15.00. The poster costs $5.00. Individualized Learning Packets (6) cost $3.00 each.

Implementation

Students are to receive classroom instruction based on IMPACT strategies two to three hours per week. Cooperative learning group activities constitute the primary format, but individualized instruction and large-group discussions are also incorporated. Activities include written reports, research projects, oral reports, art work, and drama presentations. Study sheets that accompany the lessons outline diverse instructional methodologies for the teacher's choice, with varying levels of vocabulary and task difficulty.

Teacher training involves at minimum, an intensive three-day session. IMPACT materials are available only to those who have completed the training sessions. However, one representative from a school district is eligible for training/certification to train other teachers in that same school district. Peer coaching and feedback based on observations within classrooms is part of the training process.

Level 1 training is approximately $275.00 per person, or $675.00 for a team of two teachers and their site administrator, materials are included. Level 2 training is available to Level 1 graduates appointed by the district at $375.00 per person. Technical assistance is arranged through Project IMPACT on a cost recovery basis (Winocur, 1990).

Information regarding training and materials is available from: S. Lee Winocur, National Director, IMPACT, Center for the Teaching of Thinking, 21412 Magnolia Street, Huntington Beach, CA 92646; (714) 964-3106 or from: Phi Delta Kappa, Eighth St. and Union Ave., Box 780, Bloomington, IN 47402-0789; (812) 339-1156.

Research Regarding Effectiveness

A plus for the IMPACT program is that it has been funded and sponsored by the National Diffusion Network (a division of the U.S. Department of Education) as a model program in 37 states. The program was piloted and has proliferated throughout California, one of the first states to include critical thinking on mandatory state-wide tests of basic skills.

Test results summarized from IMPACT (*Phi Delta Kappa*, 1989) indicate significant increases in reading and math scores as well as increased thinking skills as measured by the Cornell Critical Thinking Test. The research study involved approximately 700 students in grades 7–9 in four school districts. Students received thirty lessons from October 1981 to February 1982.

STRATEGIC REASONING

Overview

This program was developed by John Glade and is based on Albert Upton's (1961) *Design for Thinking* and Guilford's model of intelligence (Glade and Citron, 1985, p. 196) and Bloom's Taxonomy of Educational Objectives. The approach is described as a cognitive skills program for students from grade four through adult. The premise is that thinking skills instruction must be integrated with regular classroom learning activities. Although everyone theoretically has the capacity to perform the thinking skills identified, the ability to use them productively depends on training and experience. The six skills identified as fundamental in Strategic Reasoning involve:

(1) Thing-Making — perceiving and mentally identifying names, symbols, mental images
(2) Qualification — analyzing the characteristics of things
(3) Classification — organizing things into groups according to shared characteristics
(4) Structure Analysis — analyzing and creating part–whole relationships
(5) Operation Analysis — sequencing things, events, or thoughts into logical order
(6) Seeing Analogies — recognizing similar relationships

There are four specific goals:

(1) To build students' metacognitive abilities by developing their knowledge and use of the six fundamental thinking skills
(2) Improve students' abilities for critical thinking
(3) Develop students' abilities in verbalizing their thinking
(4) Develop students' abilities in transferring their thinking skills to nonacademic material, interdisciplinary subject matters, and real-life problem solving

Materials

Student activities progress from easy to moderate to difficult. There are three separate but related strands: (1) non-academic, (2) academic, and (3) real life. The program includes teacher strategies, problem-solving activities for students, and interdisciplinary applications. No additional materials are needed to supplement the program.

Teacher starter packages cost approximately $360.00.

Stage 1 materials consist of an 8-week multimedia kit entitled "Introducing Thinking Skills" with an accompanying "Thinking Skills Poster Set." A Teacher's Manual is included in the kit. All activities are teacher directed. Stage 1 takes about eight weeks to complete.

Stage 2 materials include skillbooks "Easy," "Medium," and "Difficult." There is also a detailed Teacher's Guide. Many of the student exercises in this stage call for divergent thinking and group discussion.

Stage 3 materials include seven skillbooks with varying reading levels. Each skillbook contains five units of academic content-based thinking instruction. Each reading selection is followed by a set of exercises called "Logic and Comprehension." The goal is for the student to transfer thinking abilities from nonacademic to academic material in a conscious yet (theoretically) natural manner.

Stage 4 materials include two multimedia instructional kits. Each kit presents a major social or emotional problem, including futuristic themes. Each kit is designed to give students the chance to use their thinking skills in personal, unstructured, real-life situations. Audio-tapes and collections of "artifacts" are included in the kits.

Approximate costs of materials: Student non-academic skillbooks, approximately $2.00 each; Student academic skillbooks, $3.50 each; Moderator's Guides, $85.00 each; Artifacts kits, $125.00 each; Thinking Skills Poster Set (6 posters), $26.00; Teacher's edition, Thinking Skills Text, $10.00; Introducing Thinking Skills Kit, $125.00.

Implementation

Target grades for mainstream teaching of thinking skills through Strategic Reasoning are 5–12. The program purportedly is also used for younger grades gifted programs, remedial retraining of thinking processes, and SAT improvement.

Formal training is optional, but available at approximately $250.00 per day from

Innovative Sciences, Inc.
P.O. Box 15129
Stamford, CT 06901-0129
(800) 243-9169
(203) 359-1311

One classroom period per week is recommended for the program.

Strategic Reasoning incorporates Upton's methodology into four stages of instruction (Glade and Citron, p. 198).

(1) Introduction to thinking skills

(2) Nonacademic thinking skill development

(3) Transfer of thinking skills to academic study

(4) Application of thinking skills to real-life problem solving

Research Regarding Effectiveness

Glade and Citron (1985, p. 202) summarize field research conducted in Washington, California, Texas, New York, and Oklahoma with students of wide ranging abilities and backgrounds. Indications are that the program has been positive in promoting students' increased performances on both standardized achievement tests (including the SAT), as well as on some IQ tests.

Zenke, in reporting specifically on the use of Strategic Reasoning in Tulsa schools, cautions that extensive prepartion and teacher training is required to implement the program properly (Zenke, 1985). A study involving middle school students indicated support for increased student performance in verbal analogies, number seriation, and figure analysis as measured on The Cognitive Abilities Test of Thorndike and Hagen (Matthews, 1989, p. 204).

TACTICS FOR THINKING

Overview

The Tactics for Thinking program is actually a set of strategies, i.e., methodology for teachers to use in integrating some twenty-two thinking skills into the "regular" curriculum. There are no separate texts for student use. The strategies are for teachers and supervisors to utilize in designing lessons for students in grades kindergarten through twelve. The strategies i.e., mental tactics of this program were developed by Robert Marzano (1986, p. 1) as a summation of theory and research on cognition, artificial intelligence, developmental psychology, information processing and other cognate fields.

The program (R. Marzano, 1985, p. 13) groups thinking skills into three main categories: (1) learning to learn skills, (2) content thinking skills, and (3) reasoning skills. In addition, there are subskills for each main category, including:

(1) Learning to learn skills (also called information processing strategies)
  a. Attention control
  b. Goal setting
  c. Monitoring attitudes
  d. Self-evaluation
(2) Content thinking skills (for acquisition of domain specific knowledge)
  a. Concept attainment
  b. Pattern recognition
  c. Synthesis
  d. Proceduralization
(3) Reasoning skills
  a. Analogical reasoning
  b. Extrapolation
  c. Evaluation of evidence
  d. Examination of value
  e. Decision making
  f. Nonlinguistic patterns
  g. Elaboration
  h. Solving everyday problems
  i. Solving academic problems
  j. Invention

Roy Forbes, as director of the Rural Education Institute, suggests that Marzano's Tactics can be an effective starting point for the integration of thinking skills throughout a school's curriculum (Forbes, 1984, p. 68). The assumption in Forbes' example is that most classroom teachers have had very little experience in the direct teaching of thinking skills and thus Marzano's program is one method of providing teachers and supervisors with an introduction to some of the terms and techniques in teaching thinking skills.

Materials

The Tactics Teacher's Manual contains 124 pages of explanations and rationales for using each technique in lesson plans and classroom activities. The cost of the manual is approximately $12.00.

The Tactics Trainer's Manual contains information for training staff developers and inservice trainers in the program. Included are 50 pages of course instructions and approximately 80 transparency masters. The Trainer's Manual costs approximately $35.00.

A preview videotape is available for a 2-day rental from ASCD (Association for Supervision and Curriculum Development) for approximately $20.00.

Implementation

The teacher's manual contains step-by-step lessons with objectives and examples listed for each teaching strategy. While not absolutely necessary, it is recommended that teachers participate in training sessions.

Workshops for training teachers/supervisors and administrators are designed for three days of intensive sessions. The sessions are designed so that those who attend are then qualified to train others in the program. The workshops with McREL personnel cost approximately $300.00. Videotapes of training sessions are also available from ASCD for approximately $545.00 purchase or $200.00 rental.

The program materials are available from

The Mid-Continent Regional Educational Laboratory (McREL)
Suite 201
125000 East Iliff Avenue
Aurora, CO 30014

or from

Association for Supervision and Curriculum Development
125 North West Street
Alexandria, VA 22314

Research Regarding Effectiveness

The program, to date, has received much press on theories of effectiveness with very little "hard" data to support its effect on student performance. Tactics was evaluated both formatively and summatively during 1984 and 1985 (Marzano, 1985, p. 13). Data were collected on seventy-seven teachers and approximately 1900 students involved in a pilot project. Conclusions of the program's positive effect on students' achievement were based on measures of teachers' observations and teacher-made tests. In general, the program produced increased student motivation, increased metacognition about task performance, and better application of content. However, the results are described as unstable, due to several limitations of the study (R. J. Marzano, 1986, p. 19).[25] Research summaries provided by McRel (1989) are based on very small samples in many cases which means that not very accurate predictions can be made about TACTICS for use in other schools.

A K–12 implementation of the program was initiated in Walla-Walla, Washington, in 1983 (Arredondo and Marzano, May, 1986, p. 28). An interesting point from this report is that several of the thinking skills as adapted for Walla-Walla schools were successful enough that some teachers wanted to develop a content-free model that all teachers could use. (That would be an application similar to the separate skills approach of CoRT and Instrumental Enrichment, among others.)

An ongoing program in incorporating Tactics involves the multi-cultural area of San Diego County, California. Approximately 1500 teachers and administrators representing forty-three school districts have completed training sessions in the program (L. King and R. King, 1988, p. 42). Conclusions regarding any research of effects on student achievement have not yet been made public.

Another ongoing program in the St. Louis, MO area involves several schools but no data are yet available regarding the effectiveness of the program (Archibald, 1990).

ENDNOTES

22. Costs of the materials currently available (estimate 10% to 30% increases for 1991 prices) have been listed in a descriptive catalogue which gives a very brief listing of each approach, the target audience, author and publisher. Research regarding implementation and/or effects on student achievement is not given, but contact with the author should provide answers to those questions. *A Catalog of Programs for Teaching Thinking*, Kruse, Janice, and Pressien, Barbara coauthors, Research for Better Schools, Inc., Philadelphia, PA, c. 1987, ERIC Document # ED 290 125.

23. For a descriptive brochure of programs endorsed by the U.S. Department of Education and disseminated through the National Diffusion Network (NDN) write Office of the Assistant Secretary for Educational Research and Improvement United States Department of Education Washington, DC 20208.

24. For more details, read *Mindstorms, Children, Computers & Powerful Ideas*, by Seymour Papert, Basic Books, Inc., New York. For a review of selected programs, see "Reviewing and Viewing," Douglas H. Clements et al. *Arithmetic Teacher*, 35(7), March 1988.

One Canadian source for information on Apple Logo, Atari Logo, IBM Logo, Coleco SmartLOGO, and Sprite LOGO, is: LOGO Computer Systems, Inc., 9960 Cote de Liesse Rd., Lachine, Quebec H8T 1A1, (514) 631-7081.

25. For further reading of Marzano's rationale in the development of Tactics for Thinking, see "Integrated Instruction in Thinking Skills, Learning Strategies, Traditional Content and Basic Beliefs: A Necessary Unity," Mid-Continent Regional Educational Lab, Aurora, Co (sponsored by U.S. Department of Education) ERIC Document # ED 267 906.

REFERENCES

ADAMS, M. 1986. "Teaching Thinking to Chapter 1 Students". In "Designs for Compensatory Education," *Conference Proceedings and Papers*. Washington, DC: ERIC Document # ED 293 913.

ARCHIBALD, G. January, 1990. Personal communication. The Network, Clayton, MO 63135.

ARREDONDO, D. and R. J. Marzano. 1986. "One District's Approach to Implementing a Comprehensive K–12 Thinking Skills Program," *Educational Leadership*, 43(8):28–30.

CHANCE, A. 1986. *Thinking in the Classroom. A Survey of Programs*. New York: Teachers College Press.

COVINGTON, M., ed. 1985. *Thinking & Learning Skills: Research and Open Questions*. Hillsdale, NJ: Lawrence Erlbaum.

CRUMP, W. D. 1988. "Teaching HOTS in the Middle and High School: A District-Level Initiative in Developing Higher-Order Thinking Skills," *Roeper Review*, 10(4):205–11.

FELDHUSEN, J. F. and P. R. Clinkenbeard. 1986. "Creativity Instructional Materials: A Review of Research," *Journal of Creative Behavior*, 20(3):153–82.

FENNELLY, P. 1988. "The Effects of One Program in Critical Thinking Instruction on the Reading Comprehension Ability of Underprepared College Students," Doctoral dissertation, State University of New York at Albany.

FORBES, R. H. 1984. "Thinking Skills: What Are They? Can They Be Taught? Why and How?" *NASSP Bulletin*, 68(476):68–75.

GLADE, J. J. and H. Citron. 1985. "Strategic Reasoning." In *Developing Minds, A Resource Book for Teaching Thinking*, A. Costa, ed. Alexandria, VA: Association for Supervision and Curriculum Development, pp. 196–202.

HARRIS, D. G. and S. S. Blank. 1983. "A Comparative Study: Two Approaches to Enhance Creative Problem-Solving in Grade Five Students," *British Columbia Journal of Special Education*, 7(2):129–52.

HOTS Information Pamphlet. 1989. Tucson, AZ: Thinking with Computers.

KING, L. and R. King. 1988. "Tactics for Thinking in Action," *Educational Leadership*, 45(7):42–44.

MARZANO, R. 1985. *Impact Report: December 1, 1984–November 30, 1985*. ERIC

Document # ED 266 539. St. Louis, MO: Mid-Continent Regional Educational Lab., Inc.

MARZANO, R. J. 1986. *An Evaluation of the McREL Thinking Skills Program.* ERIC Document # ED 267 907. Aurora, CO: Mid-Continent Regional Educational Laboratory.

MARZANO, R. J. 1989. Summary Report: Evaluation of the Tactics for Thinking Program. Aurora, CO: Mid Continent Regional Educational Laboratory.

MATTHEWS, D. B. 1989. "The Effects of a Thinking Skills Program on the Cognitive Abilities of Middle School Students," *The Clearing House*, 62(5): 202–204.

NEWMAN, J. M. 1988. "Online: LOGO and the Language Arts," *Language Arts*, 65(6):598–605.

NICKERSON, R., D. Perkins and E. Smith. 1985. *The Teaching of Thinking.* Hillsdale, NJ: Lawrence Erlbaum Associates.

PHI DELTA KAPPA. 1989. *IMPACT*, information brochure. Bloomington, IN: Phi Delta Kappa.

POGROW, S. 1985. "HOTS: A Computer-Based Approach." In *Developing Minds, A Resource Book for Teaching Thinking*, A. Costa, ed. Alexandria, WA: Association for Supervision and Curriculum Development, pp. 239–240.

POGROW, S. July 1990. Personal communication.

POGROW, S. 1988. "Teaching Thinking to At-Risk Elementary Students," *Educational Leadership*, 45(7):79–85.

POGROW, S. 1990. "A Socratic Approach to Using Computers with At-Risk Students," *Educational Leadership*, pp. 61–66.

ROBINSON, L. 1984. *Where Does LOGO Fit In?* Paper presented at a meeting of the National Association of Laboratory Schools. Chicago, IL: ERIC Document Reproduction Services # ED 278 379.

SATTLER, D. M. 1987. *Programming in BASIC or LOGO: Effects on Critical Thinking Skills* (Doctoral dissertation, University of New Mexico).

SEGAL, J. and S. Chipman, eds. 1985. *Thinking and Learning Skills: Research and Open Questions.* Hillsdale, NJ: Lawrence Erlbaum.

SHULIK, J. P. 1988. "Project IMPACT in Elementary Schools," *Educational Leadership*, 45(7):41.

WHIMBEY, A. 1985. "Test Results from Teaching Thinking." In *Developing Minds, a Resource Book for Teaching Thinking*, A. Costa, ed. Alexandria, VA: Association for Supervision and Curriculum Development, pp. 169–271.

WHIMBEY, A. 1984. "The Key to Higher Order Thinking is Precise Processing," *Educational Leadership*, 42(1):66–70.

WHIMBEY, A. and J. Lockhead. 1980. *Problem Solving and Comprehension, a Short Course in Analytical Reasoning.* Philadelphia: The Franklin Institute Press.

WIEDERHOLD, C. 1985. "Uses of Computers for Teaching Thinking." In *Developing Minds, A Resource Book for Teaching Thinking*, A. Costa, ed. Alexandria, VA: Association for Supervision and Curriculum Development.

WINOCUR, S. L. 1985. "Project Impact." In *Developing Minds, a Resource Book for Teaching Thinking*, A. Costa, ed. Alexandria, VA: Association for Supervision and Curriculum Development, pp. 210–211.

WINOCUR, S. L. July 1990. Personal communication.

WRIGHT, E. 1985. "Odyssey: A Curriculum for Thinking." In *Developing Minds, a Resource Book for Teaching Thinking*, A. Costa, ed. Alexandria, VA: Association for Supervision and Curriculum Development, pp. 224–226.

ZENKE, L. 1985. *Improving School Effectiveness by Teaching Thinking Skills.* Papre presented at the Annual Meeting of the American Association of School Administrators. EPIC Document # ED 257 197.

Editorials

POSITION PAPER
BY J. R. BANKS

Weigh the evidence and be bold! To continue the excessive dependence on rote-memory activities in schools is outdated. The evidence, whether statistical or anecdotal, strongly favors the direct teaching of thinking skills. The evidence supports the adoption of pre-existing programs, rather than to attempt the massive retraining of teachers for teaching thinking skills. A strong caution is inserted, however, in that not all materials with the words critical thinking in the title or description, actually teach critical thinking. At last count, some 500 publications were advertised as materials to teach or support critical thinking in public schools (1989 RBS Project Brief).

The tendency all too often in schools is to take a "quick-fix" approach to whatever deficiencies have been targeted for remediation. A "quick-fix" approach will not work with teaching thinking skills any more than a quick-fix course would produce a proficient pilot, musician, chef, writer, or computer technician. The time and effort involved are directly proportional to the success of a program. Although the effort is great, the enthusiasm of teachers, students, parents, and administrators is strongly supportive of the long-term benefits of many of the well-documented programs.

Many of the programs require in-service training of teachers. Attempts to use those programs without the training of teachers and administrators has not been positive. In other words, in order to use the good programs, a school cannot simply order the materials as if adopting another new textbook. Training is an essential element in the correct use of thinking skills materials. Thus, the initial cost may be high but most of the materials are reusable and training for consecutive years' usage in a program is usually much less than for the first year.

An honest attempt has been made to search the literature for independently publicized reports of research for each program discussed in this book. Many ongoing projects simply have not been in existence long enough to adequately measure results. A minimum of two years is necessary for even cautious conclusions as to a program's effectiveness.

Those with positive *or* negative experiences to share in any approach to teaching thinking skills, whether with pre-packaged programs or generic strategies, are encouraged to write to the author at the following address.

> East Tennessee State University
> Department of Curriculum and Instruction
> Box 23,020A
> Johnson City, TN 37604-0002

INSTRUMENTAL ENRICHMENT AT LAUREL HIGH SCHOOL BY MARY OLIVER[26]

The fundamental principle on which Laurel High School was organized and continues to operate is that a school should promote the personal characteristics of successful human beings: the ability to cooperate, evaluate, and make decisions; curiosity, enthusiasm, and reliability; an inner sense of competence; and concern for others. We constantly test new approaches to learning which foster the growth of these characteristics, retaining those that work.

Although it is well-known that creativity sometimes comes in awkward packages, the large, conventional school finds itself unable to tolerate widely different styles of learning and must confine itself to the median. Independent-minded students—who may have done well everywhere except in school—can be successful in our more flexible learning environment.

During the first ten of the eighteen years Laurel High School has operated, we enjoyed support from the National Endowment for the Arts for a comprehensive art program. We have continued the core of this program but have not been able to continue scholarships in art or the young teacher–artist program.

Entrance requirement: willingness to engage in constructive learning activity.

Graduation requirement: 20 units; progress toward graduation measured by class-equivalents which are based on student/teacher evaluation of what has been accomplished.

Graduates: college, 80%; employed or operating own business, 20%; students are encouraged to formulate career goals and to plan their education accordingly.

Enrollment: limited to 30.

Teachers: 12 (full-time equivalent: 4)

Tuition: $2090/year, payable monthly; Building Fund contribution requested.

Location: The school is based in a fourteen-room renovated house near the Knoxville campus of the University of Tennessee.

The first section of the Instrumental Enrichment program was introduced during the first week of school to all students enrolled at that time. Thereafter, students were self-paced, working on the sheets in math classes or during freetime.

After four months of school, one student has completed all the instruments we have (Organization of Dots, Orientation in Space I, Comparisons, Analytic Preception); others have completed some instruments and are working on others. A few are avoiding doing the pages unless they are in need of class-equivalents (since our students must earn at least 25 class-equivalents per week, some students use the IE sheets to fill a gap).

Student Comments

"I like dots."

"Very mind-teasing—makes you think."

"Good for improving study skills."

"A fun creativity of progressive strategy and thinking."

"I like them especially when I have nothing else to do. They exercise your brain."

"I think they're neat! I think they're totally tubular. They really keep me occupied and they're very interesting."

"They're really not that bad."

In addition to the above positive comments, four students had no comments about the program, and four students had negative remarks in language not suitable for the classroom.

Teacher Comments:

"These exercises focus attention of the student; they help in sustaining concentration."

"The work sheets seem to help students to analyze and synthesize information."

"I have noticed students completing the dot-connecting forms at various times throughout the semester, particularly during leisure time. Since my suggestions for leisure-time activities generally go unheeded, I infer that the students involved see these activities as meaningful, all the more so since they will work on the forms until they are fully completed."

PHILOSOPHY FOR CHILDREN IN UNIVERSITY CITY SCHOOLS
BY DAVE ACKERMAN[27]

During the 1985–86 school year the Superintendent of schools asked me, in my role as Director of Math, Science, and Computer Curriculum, to investigate the various thinking skills programs available and make a recommendation to him concerning the district's future commitments in this area. The central office staff was committed to change. Years of a back-to-basics philosophy had left us with a curriculum steeped in workbooks, unsettling test scores for minority children, a test-driven instructional program, poor student language skills, and a realization that too many students could not use the basic skills they had been taught.

I undertook the task with tremendous zeal because I believed that a thinking skills program could breathe life into our curriculum. Believing that change needed to occur quickly and not be slowed down by the usual political bureaucratic processes, I began, carried out and ended my investigations as a committee of one. I went through the alphabet soup of CoRT, HOTS, IMPACT, TACTICS, Socratic dialogue, . . . and Philosophy for Children. I went to several conferences and read Glaser, Feuerstein, Costa, Marzano, Perkins, Black, Beyer, . . . and Lipman. When my journey ended I believed that Philosophy for Children was the thinking skills program for the University City School System.

The superintendent of schools was convinced that Philosophy for Children was the program for our district because of its ability to help us on many fronts. The program teaches several transferable thinking skills, including sorting relevant from irrelevant, accuracy, ambiguity, assumptions, bias, and detection of fallacies. The program pulls teachers out of their teacher's guides and involves them in thinking about their own thinking, their students' thinking, planning for thinking, and improving their questioning techniques. The stories that initiate the classroom discussions are heavily values–ethics laden, something missing from our present program. And most importantly, the program depends heavily on developing oral language abilities increasing the students' abilities to express, defend, and expand their own ideas and beliefs.

Philosophy for Children was to become the district's thinking skills program. We piloted the program in several classes, pre- and post-testing students using the New Jersey Test of Reasoning. Our test results were very positive. Results were shared with principals and schools were invited to participate. Teachers in the schools volunteered on an individual and in some cases grade level basic. Training and materials were provided the following year – the Philosophy for Children program was a reality. Of our six elementary schools, four had some level of participation.

That next year I became a principal. I came to my school filled with the knowledge of what this program could do for children. I "informed" my staff that we would be trained and that we would initiate Philosophy for Children. As a new principal I did not meet with much resistance, but indeed the program was "mine." I had identified the needs, done the investigation of available programs, and I had made the decision to implement. My new staff came along because they felt they had to. Teachers gave the program good reviews as we went through the first two years; however, in the two years since, only one teacher uses the program on a regular basis.

What happened? Certainly the top down decision making played a major role in the lack of sustained commitment. In addition, as the school has grown and changed we have had a 50% turnover in staff. Each year one, two or three new staff members have been added, causing a real logistical problem trying to provide training. I believe the other major factor has to do with the nature of elementary education. 1986 was our "year" for thinking skills, 1987 was our "year" for science education, 1988 was for drug education, 1989 was multicultural education, 1990 is early childhood education, and 1991 may be the crisis in geography. Sustaining emphasis, training, evaluation, and revision with new ideas and programs is so difficult when each year another program, no matter how valid, is introduced. Our ability to concentrate the efforts needed to make a new program a part of our everyday thinking and behavior is next to impossible with the never ending lists of things to be emphasized.

Presently, the one teacher who uses Philosophy for Children consistently does so for all the reasons I have previously listed. She believes in the program and believes that it indeed develops critical thinking and oral language ability. She believes that it helps students use the basic skills they are being taught and improves their standardized test scores.

Elsewhere in the district the program has reached an institutionalized status at the Sixth Grade Center School. There the program is offered as an elective and approximately 150 students each year are enrolled. The junior high-type setting there has allowed for this level of acceptance. Only a few teachers had to be trained. Philosophy for Children is scheduled in specific time slots and does not have to compete for time with reading, math, etc. Its presence in the course book and its elective status has given it acceptance and positive recommendations.

If I were to go down this road again, I believe I would sacrifice time and experience for grass roots involvement and ownership. I believe that even with all the competing issues we must address that Philosophy for Children could have endured and flourished as a regular component of our curriculum.

THE COLLEGE CONNECTION
BY LAURA BARNETT[28]

In July of 1988 I conducted a survey of twenty-five southeastern universities in order to assess the curricular focus in second semester English courses. The twenty-five universities represented the entire population of moderate-sized southeastern universities operating on the semester system. Of the twenty-five universities selected, nineteen responded for a response rate of 76 percent.

The data were grouped into two categories: literature-based and non-literature-based. Of the non-literature based group, 50% included argument/persuasion as required skills to be taught. Of the literature-based group, 25% indicated persuasion/argument skills as required skills in the course. Although the word "analysis" was not listed as a specific skill in the questionnaire, 25% of the respondents listed analysis as a matter of concern. Other terms which indicate critical thinking are "an extended critical paper" (University of Louisville), "sharpen critical reading skills" (Western Kentucky University), "concentrate on persuasion and argument" (Northwestern State University of Louisiana and Louisiana State University), "research/argument core" (East Carolina University), "research paper/critical paper" (Southeastern Louisiana University), and "write critically about" (Northern Kentucky University).

Findings from the study indicate that a significant number of respondents, 56 percent, are using a relatively non-literature-based content in their second semester freshman English courses. The implication is that the skills stressed in these courses require more independent student thought in analysis, i.e., critical thinking. Traditionally, courses which are literature-based develop skills in comprehension and some analysis, but less depth in critical analysis, which includes student opinion. The usual format is for the professor to lecture about a particular author's work from the point of view of "experts'" interpretation. However, in courses which are non-literature based, it becomes the student who chooses sources to support his/her argument, an exercise which requires more in-depth analysis of student's thought than merely accepting the professor's or other "experts'" arguments.

This survey pertained to second-semester college English courses. It is encouraging to find 75 percent of the courses require argument/persuasion. Argument/persuasion in this sense is a "generic" thinking skill. An obvious factor relating to student success for these courses is to have students entering college with extensive practice in thinking skills. As to the best way to prepare those students, that remains a conclusion for the pre-college schools to make. It may be that utilizing a specific thinking skills program in early grades which teaches skills that are readily transferable to writing across the curriculum-type programs or other composition courses in senior high schools will prove to be a logical sequence. Historically, teachers of pre-college English courses in high school have utilized little persuasion/analysis in their courses. The implications are that it is past time to do so.

STRUCTURE OF INTELLECT IN BULADEAN ELEMENTARY SCHOOL BY L. G. SHEETS, RESOURCE TEACHER[29]

Buladean is a K–8 elementary school in the Mitchell, North Carolina public school system. Prior to the 1987–88 school year, the Director of Special Education informed the Special Education faculty that he had discovered a great program that we would be using in our classes in the coming year. That program was Meeker's "Structure of Intellect". We teachers dutifully took our materials back to our classrooms and proceeded to implement the program. We thought. Personally, I found it difficult to understand and thus difficult to explain some of the activities to students, particularly the color coding. Students frequently complained that many of the activities were too easy and they couldn't understand the need for doing them. Other teachers in the district have expressed similar difficulties with implementing the program. Later, I found out that there is a minimum of training recommended for teachers prior to any attempts to use the program with students. We teachers did not receive the formal training, nor did the Director of Special Education receive the training, due to the usual budget constraints.

To make a long story short, trying to implement the program without background information and training was not cost-effective. In trying to save money, the district was short-sighted. I do not know of any teachers in our school system using the materials at this point.

ENDNOTES

26. Mary Oliver, B.A., M.A., Pennsylvania State University, was Head of the Mathematics Department at Ellis School, Pittsburgh (grades 9 through 12) where she devised a math program for kindergarten through grade 12. Upon moving to Knoxville, Tennessee, in 1969, she became active in establishing the Knoxville Corporation, an umbrella corporation under which groups interested in alternatives to conventional education could organize. Ms. Oliver helped to organize Laurel High School as part of the Knoxville School Corporation and has taught mathematics, physical sciences, and assorted other subjects as requested by students during the succeeding eighteen years.

27. Dave Ackerman has been principal of Delmar-Harvard Elementary School since September 1986. Prior to that time he was Director of Math Science and Computer Curriculum for the University City Public Schools and was an elementary classroom teacher for fifteen years prior to that. Delmar-Harvard is an urban elementary school with 330 students, 75 percent African-American, 20 percent White, and 5 percent from various foreign countries. The socioeconomic status ranges from very poor to upper middle-class. University City is a suburb of St. Louis, Missouri.

28. Laura Barnett has taught English and General Speech at Northeast Tennessee Community College and East Tennessee State University. Currently she is a doctoral fellow in Leadership and Policy Analysis at East Tennessee State University.

29. L. G. Sheets is a resource teacher, providing additional instruction to selected students, primarily in Language Arts and Mathematics. He is a Masters candidate at East Tennessee State University, Johnson City.

REFERENCES

BRELL, C. D., JR. 1990. "Critical Thinking as Transfer: The Reconstructive Integration of Otherwise Descrete Interpretations of Experience," *Educational Theory*, 40(1):53–68.

COLLINS, C. 1989. "Administrators Can Increase Their Students' Higher-Level Thinking Abilities," *Clearinghouse*, 62(9):391–396.

Research for Better Schools Project Brief. 1989. No. 2.

APPENDIX

Instruments Used for Assessing Critical Thinking Skills:

Cornell Critical Thinking Test, Level X. 1985. Ennis, R. H. and J. Millman, Midwest Publications, P.O. Box 448, Pacific Grove, CA 93950. Target grades: 4–14. Contains 76 items: timed or untimed.

Cornell Critical Thinking Test, Level Z. 1985. Ennis, R. and J. Millman, Midwest Publications, P.O. Box 448, Pacific Grove, CA 93950. Target grades: Gifted, or advanced high school students, college students, adults.

Ennis-Weir Critical Thinking Essay Test. 1985. Ennis, R. and E. Weir, Midwest Publications, P.O. Box 448, Pacific Grove, CA 93950. Target grades: 7–adult.

New Jersey Test of Reasoning Skills. 1983. Shipman, V. IAPC Test Division, Montclair State College, Upper Montclair, NJ 08403. Target grades: 4–college. Contains 50 items, untimed.

Ross Test of Higher Cognitive Processes. 1976. Ross, J. D. and C. Ross, Academic Therapy Publications, 20 Commercial Blvd., Novato, CA 94947.

Watson-Glaser Critical Thinking Appraisal. 1980. Watson, Goodwin, and Glaser. The Psychological Corporation Division of Harcourt Brace Jovanovich, 7500 Old Oak Blvd., Cleveland, OH 44130.

Whimbey Analytical Skills Inventory. WASI. Available through course textbook, *Problem Solving and Comprehension*, by A. Whimbey and J. Lockhead, Lawrence Erlbaum, Inc., 365 Broadway, Hillsdale, NJ 07642.

ENDNOTES

1. "Knowing Is Not Thinking" by E. Janko, *Phi Delta Kappan*, March, 1989, pp. 543–544, and "Commentary, The 3 R's: Reading, Writing, and Reasoning" by J. Howard, April 22, 1987 *Education Week*, p. 23.

2. Robert Sternberg is a Yale psychologist who has written extensively about intelligence and thinking skills.

3. Robert Ennis is Director of the Illinois Critical Thinking Project and Professor of Philosophy, Department of Educational Policy Studies, University of Illinois at Urbana-Champaign.

4. David Perkins is Co-Director of Harvard University's Project Zero and author of extensive articles about creative and critical thinking.

5. A very thorough examination of the testing issue can be found in the October, 1985 issue of *Educational Leadership*. Sixteen articles present various aspects of the problems involved in schools testing of students.

6. For more details, two sources are recommended: *Guidelines for Preparing the Research Proposal* by J. H. Behling and *The Process of Grant Proposal Development*, Phi Delta Kappa Fastback #143. A more detailed source is *Making It Happen, Designing Research with Implementation in Mind* by M. Hakel, et al.

7. Personal communication, October, 1986.

8. For a thorough explanation of the program, see *Philosophy in the Classroom* by Matthew Lipman, Ann Margaret Sharp, and Frederick S. Oscanyan.

9. The students are not supposed to be formally graded on their performance/participation in the program. Lipman contends that this would lead to a teacher-centered discussion, which is contrary to the essence of developing of improved student thinking. I have not encountered teachers who find this lack of grading a problem, once they get students trained in the discussion format of the program.

10. More detailed descriptions of the materials and training options are available by writing to the Institute for the Advancement of Philosophy for Children, Montclair State College, Upper Montclair, NJ 07043. There are also several other books, two newsletters (one for the U.S. and one international), and a scholarly-type yet readable journal about the program available from the IAPC.

11. This perceptual measure as identified by Witkin is called field-dependence/independence and is measured by the "Group Embedded Figures Test." A readable summary of this research is included in *Marching to Different Drummers* by Pat Burke Guild and Stephen Garger, published by ASCD (1985).

12. Descriptions of the programs are only briefly summarized here. For more information contact Dr. Frances R. Link, Curriculum Development Associates, Inc., Suite 414, 1211 Connecticut Avenue, NW, Washington, DC 20036.

13. In the closing remarks in the Foreward of *Teaching Thinking*, the reader is instructed to "take from the book whatever constructive ideas he may find rather than regarding it as a source of philosophical points with which he can enjoy disagreeing." This reflects a tone which often runs through de Bono's works. CoRT has been adapted by Sydney Tyler, in cooperation with Dr. de Bono, for use in U.S. Department of Defense Schools in pre-school and elementary classrooms. This adaptation is used in several districts in the U.S. and Canada. Called *Just Think* and *Stretch Think*, information regarding this series is available through: Thomas Geale Publications, Inc., 1142 Manhattan Avenue, Drawer C. P. 223, Manhattan Beach, CA 90266, (213) 379-4405.

14. de Bono has written extensively about his theories of thinking. If one book were chosen to read as background to his program, *Teaching Thinking* is probably the most thorough yet fairly readable.

15. I have found that in personal interviews, teachers who use CoRT are quite enthusiastic despite the lack of statistical analysis of effectiveness of thinking skills as taught through CoRT.

16. In one instance, teachers in Moose Jaw, Saskatchewan, utilized a satellite hookup and video interaction for workshop training.

17. For a descriptive brochure and current prices of materials, write to Dormac, Inc., P.O. Box 270459, San Diego, CA 92128-0983, (800) 547-8032 or Dominie Press Limited, 1361 Agincourt, Ontario M1S 3J1, Canada.

18. For information about the program and training, write to SOI Systems, P.O. Box D, Vida, OR 97488, (503) 896-3936.

19. A personal conversation with one psychometrist (B.A. and M.Ed. in counseling) indicated a disagreement with this conclusion; she indicated that SOI screening devices are much easier and more objective for her purposes in individualized tutoring programs.

20. This "major" ability is rarely included as a part of school curriculum, according to Meeker (p. 7). This is the portion of the SOI program involving activities most similar to other thinking skills programs.

21. A counselor or psychologist versed in testing procedures would find it advisable to read Meeker's (1969) *Structure of Intellect, Its Interpretation and Uses* as minimal background information regarding the program and testing rationale.

22. Costs of the materials currently available (estimate 10% to 30% increases for 1991 prices) have been listed in a descriptive catalogue which gives a very brief listing of each approach, the target audience, author and publisher.

Research regarding implementation and/or effects on student achievement is not given, but contact with the author should provide answers to those questions. *A Catalog of Programs for Teaching Thinking*, Kruse, Janice, and Pressien, Barbara coauthors, Research for Better Schools, Inc., Philadelphia, PA, c. 1987, ERIC Document # ED 290 125.

23. For a descriptive brochure of programs endorsed by the U.S. Department of Education and disseminated through the National Diffusion Network (NDN) write Office of the Assistant Secretary for Educational Research and Improvement United States Department of Education Washington, DC 20208.

24. For more details, read *Mindstorms, Children, Computers & Powerful Ideas*, by Seymour Papert, Basic Books, Inc., New York. For a review of selected programs, see "Reviewing and Viewing," Douglas H. Clements et al. *Arithmetic Teacher*, 35(7), March 1988.

One Canadian source for information on Apple Logo, Atari Logo, IBM Logo, Coleco SmartLOGO, and Sprite LOGO, is: LOGO Computer Systems, Inc., 9960 Cote de Liesse Rd., Lachine, Quebec H8T 1A1, (514) 631-7081.

25. For further reading of Marzano's rationale in the development of Tactics for Thinking, see "Integrated Instruction in Thinking Skills, Learning Strategies, Traditional Content and Basic Beliefs: A Necessary Unity," Mid-Continent Regional Educational Lab, Aurora, Co (sponsored by U.S. Department of Education) ERIC Document # ED 267 906.

26. Mary Oliver, B.A., M.A., Pennsylvania State University, was Head of the Mathematics Department at Ellis School, Pittsburgh (grades 9 through 12) where she devised a math program for kindergarten through grade 12. Upon moving to Knoxville, Tennessee, in 1969, she became active in establishing the Knoxville Corporation, an umbrella corporation under which groups interested in alternatives to conventional education could organize. Ms. Oliver helped to organize Laurel High School as part of the Knoxville School Corporation and has taught mathematics, physical sciences, and assorted other subjects as requested by students during the succeeding eighteen years.

27. Dave Ackerman has been principal of Delmar-Harvard Elementary School since September 1986. Prior to that time he was Director of Math Science and Computer Curriculum for the University City Public Schools and was an elementary classroom teacher for fifteen years prior to that. Delmar-Harvard is an urban elementary school with 330 students, 75 percent African-American, 20 percent White, and 5 percent from various foreign countries. The socioeconomic status ranges from very poor to upper middle-class. University City is a suburb of St. Louis, Missouri.

28. Laura Barnett has taught English and General Speech at Northeast Tennessee Community College and East Tennessee State University. Currently she is a doctoral fellow in Leadership and Policy Analysis at East Tennessee State University.

29. L. G. Sheets is a resource teacher, providing additional instruction to selected students, primarily in Language Arts and Mathematics. He is a Masters candidate at East Tennessee State University, Johnson City.

GLOSSARY

analytical thinking — to examine in detail, all aspects of a problem

cognition — the process of knowing

convergent — to come to a similar point of view

creative thinking — the generation of new possibilities

critical thinking — thinking that is focused on strategies for deciding what to believe or do

deductive reasoning — from the general to the specific

dialectic teaching — involving spoken language in the form of dialogue among students and teacher(s)

didactic teaching — teacher-directed, focused on convergent thinking

divergent thinking — to branch off into different possibilities

educable mentally retarded — students of below average cognitive abilities

ethics — critical analysis of moral concepts in both public and private life

generic thinking skills — generalized terms for thinking skills which can theoretically be taught in all school subjects (across the curriculum)

higher-order thinking — complex levels of thought requiring more mental processing than mere recall of rote-momorized details

hypothesis — an unproved theory that is based on logical possibility

inductive reasoning — from particular, specific facts to general conclusions

inference — reasoning from something known or assumed

inquiry — to ask questions and investigate; to seek information about the question

learning disability—a condition that inhibits the mental processing of information (not associated in any way with measures of IQ)

literacy—the ability to read and write on a "normal" adult level

logic—what is demonstrated to follow from premises that are evidenced as true

mainstreaming—educating handicapped students in the least restrictive school setting

metacognition—the ability to reflect on our own thinking (awareness of what we do and do not know)

metaphor—a figure of speech where one thing is said as if it were another

mnemonic device—an aid to memorization

philosophy—study of the principles underlying thought; thinking about thinking

reasoning—to think analytically

rudiment—a first-level principle

simile—a figure of speech comparing one thing to another by using "like" or "as"

thinking skills—knowing how to use the resources of language

transfer (bridging)—to use the skill taught in one subject area in a different subject area

value statement—a statement of "fact" based on personal beliefs and standards

INDEX

109